Stringing
Beaded Jewelry

Stringing
Beaded Jewelry

Karin Buckingham

KALMBACH BOOKS

Kalmbach Books
21027 Crossroads Circle
Waukesha, Wisconsin 53186
www.Kalmbach.com/Books

Published in 2010
14 13 12 11 10   1 2 3 4 5

Manufactured in the United States of America

ISBN: 978-0-87116-299-1

Publisher's Cataloging-in-Publication Data
Buckingham, Karin.
  Stringing beaded jewelry / Karin Buckingham.

    p. : col. ill. ; cm. — (The absolute beginners guide)

  Subtitle from cover: Everything you need to know to get started
  ISBN: 978-0-87116-299-1

1. Beadwork—Handbooks, manuals, etc. 2. Jewelry making—Handbooks, manuals, etc. I. Title.

TT860 .B83 2010
745.594/2

Contents

Introduction 6

Basics 7

Stringing Projects 18

PROJECT**1** Simple strung necklace 20

PROJECT**2** Pattern with two bead sizes ... 22

PROJECT**3** Pattern with more differentiation ... 24

PROJECT**4** Necklace of graduated beads ... 26

PROJECT**5** Center focus 28

PROJECT**6** Center dangle 30

PROJECT**7** Simple multistrand necklace and bracelet ... 32

PROJECT**8** Graduated-length multistrand necklace ... 34

PROJECT**9** Multistrand necklace with centered pendant ... 36

PROJECT**10** Short asymmetrical necklace ... 38

PROJECT**11** Long asymmetrical necklace ... 40

PROJECT**12** Bead soup bracelet 42

PROJECT**13** Stretch-cord bracelet 44

PROJECT**14** Multistrand stretch-cord bracelet ... 46

Connecting Projects 48

PROJECT15 Easy chain bracelet 50

PROJECT16 Wrapped-loop earrings 52

PROJECT17 Chain necklace with dangles 54

PROJECT18 Dangle earrings 56

PROJECT19 Plain-loop earrings 58

PROJECT20 Dangle pendant with earrings 60

PROJECT21 Cluster bracelet 62

Fiber Fun 64

PROJECT22 Knotting pearls 66

PROJECT23 Knotting a big-bead necklace 68

PROJECT24 Simple pendant on silk ribbon 70

PROJECT25 Suede cord plus chain
with dangles 72

PROJECT26 Beaded leather cord 74

PROJECT27 Multistrand cord necklace 76

PROJECT28 Wire mesh necklace 78

PROJECT29 Two easy adjustable closures 80

Extra Goodies 82

PROJECT30 Chain extender with dangle 84

PROJECT31 Toggle closure extender 85

PROJECT32 Headpins from wire scraps 86

PROJECT33 Simple earring wires 87

PROJECT34 Clasp assortment 88

PROJECT35 Beading work board 90

Top 10 Stringing Techniques 91

Top 10 Creativity Tips 94

Resources
From the Author 95

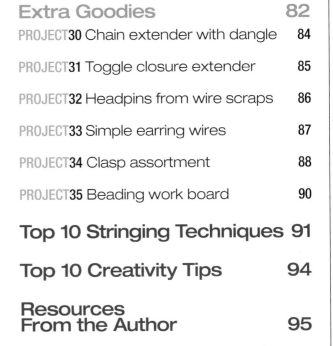

Introduction

Have you had a "can't help myself" moment in the bead aisle of your craft store, or as you viewed the tempting strands at your local bead store? Do you have a small stash of sparklies, and now you're wondering, "Just what am I going to do with these?" You're hooked, but you're just not sure what to do next.

This book is for you. As you work through the projects, you'll be introduced to the building blocks of bead stringing as well as a few very simple wireworking and knotting techniques. You'll explore using exciting materials including chain, suede, and metal mesh. You'll learn how to make necklaces, bracelets, and earrings. In "Another Idea," you'll get a suggestion for improvising on the project if you're feeling adventurous. Along the way, you'll learn and practice fundamental stringing skills: strong and secure crimps; nice, round loops; well-draped strands; smoothly connected jump rings; and a perfect fit every time. Soon they'll become second nature.

Each project section—Stringing, Connecting, Fiber Fun, and Extra Goodies—begins with the most basic information. You may want to try the first few projects in each section before you move on to the others; working through or at least reading every project in the book will help you build a fantastic stringing skill set. Basic skills are introduced in the projects (look for the line at the top of the page to see what you'll be learning) and repeated again in my "Top 10 Techniques" at the end of the book for a handy reference, should you need a review.

Don't worry too much about the specific beads I've used. You're learning techniques, and it really doesn't matter if you use the same beads or not. Choose colors, shapes, and textures that you love, and follow my directions and step-by-step photos. We'll make a perfect team!

Basics

All you need to make beautiful jewelry is beads, something to string them on, and maybe a clasp. Sounds easy, right? Easy until you walk into a bead store for the first time, that is. Where do you start? Which beads do you choose? What do you really need to begin?

The short answer is, "Buy what you love and what fits in your budget." If it's pretty to you, it doesn't really matter if it's a one-of-a-kind art bead or something that was mass produced. If this answer fits, you may be ready to move right to the projects, which begin on p. 18. Glance at the "must-haves" that follow, and come back to this section at your leisure.

But the longer answer is "understand what you're looking at, and use that knowledge to help you make buying decisions." The following visual glossary is intended to help you get familiar with all of the essentials that make up the wonderful world of bead stringing.

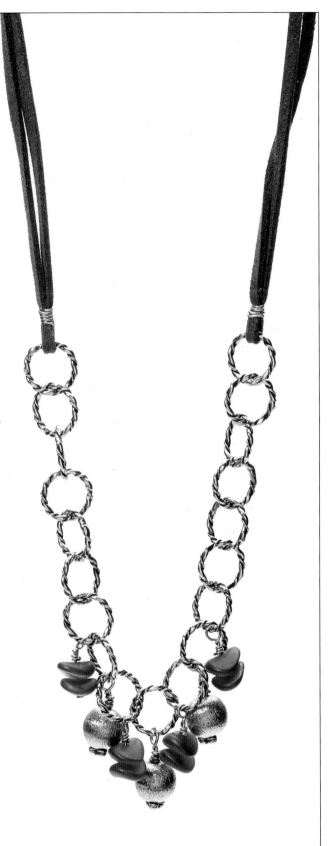

BEADS

Gold-filled, sterling silver, plated, and base-metal (nonprecious metal) beads can be found in many sizes, textures, and shapes. **Spacer beads** are "helper" beads that accent a focal bead or extend a pattern. **Spacer bars** with several holes keep multiple strands aligned. **Bali-style** beads are characterized by patterns created with tiny balls of silver and black oxidation in the recesses. **Hill Tribes silver** beads are handmade in Thailand, often incorporate natural themes and rustic decoration, and have a light color that's due to their high silver content.

Precision-cut crystals add sparkle and flash to your beading designs. Their lead content gives them weight, depth, and clarity unlike any other type of glass or crystal. The most well-known and high-quality crystals for beading are made in Austria and are branded as Crystallized Swarovski Elements, with many choices of shapes, colors, and finishes. Swarovski also manufactures a line of glass pearl beads. These high-quality pearls are perfectly sized and have a beautiful weight and finish.

Seed beads are small glass beads that come in a wide array of colors, finishes, sizes, and shapes (although the most common shape is round). Devotees of seed beads stitch them with needle and thread into complex jewelry. For stringing purposes, they make excellent spacers and are an easy way to add splashes of color to your design. Common sizes range from the tiny size 15, sometimes seen as 15° (say "fifteen aught") to the much larger 6°, with 11° being a popular size. **Cylinder beads**, a subset of seed beads often from Japan, are uniform in size and have straight, even edges like tiny tubes. You'll often find them packaged in tubes or other small containers, sometimes identified with their weight in grams. **Round seed beads** sold on hanks (many strands tied together) come from the Czech Republic. They are more irregular than Japanese seed beads, so they have a more textural appearance. **Bugle beads** are very narrow tubes, either smooth or twisted. Seed beads are also available in cube, triangle, teardrop, and other shapes.

Cultured freshwater pearls provide organic beauty and deep luster. Many have been dyed to achieve a broad range of colors. It's a good idea to soak pearls in water to help remove excess dye before you string them. Shapes include round, rice, rondelle, potato, keishi, stick, and coin.

Gemstone beads are formed from natural rocks such as quartz, garnet, amazonite, turquoise, and many more. Shapes include nuggets, rounds, ovals, rectangles, and rondelles, and finishes can be smooth, faceted, or natural. Some gemstones are dyed to enhance or change the color. Look carefully as you select, and ask for help if you have questions about whether a stone is natural or enhanced. Gemstones are usually sold on a 15- or 16-in. (38 or 41 cm) strand, which is usually enough for one necklace or several bracelets (especially if you mix in accent beads and other components).

For centuries, people have made creative use of **natural materials** found in their environment, shaping beads and adornments from wood, bones, nuts, shells, and seeds.

Beads made from **Lucite, plastic, and resin** can be new or vintage. Lucite is a trademarked type of acrylic resin; vintage Lucite beads can be highly collectable. Plastic beads are an inexpensive way to get started in this hobby, and jewelry made with lightweight plastic is comfortable to wear. Resin beads, also lightweight, are cast into a variety of colorful shapes and sizes. **Polymer clay beads** can be elaborate, whimsical, or anywhere in between. Lightweight polymer beads add color and pattern to jewelry.

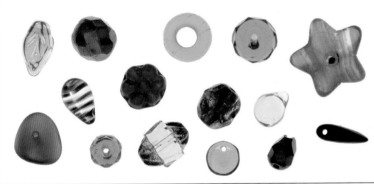

Glass and crystal beads from the Czech Republic are available in many shapes and sizes. **Fire-polished** means the crystals have been heat-finished to give them a colorful, iridescent glow. A **cathedral bead** has paned edges and often has gilding or other color at the tip. Czech beads can also be round or rondelle (a slightly flattened round). Czech **pressed-glass beads** are molded shapes such as daggers, disks, flowers, or leaves.

The shimmery colors in **dichroic glass beads** come from ultra-thin layers of metals that are fused with glass.

Lampworked beads are made one at a time by heating glass in a torch flame until it is molten and shaping it around rods.

Furnace glass is known for its candy-like bright colors and playful shapes. Bands of colored glass are encased in a clear outer layer, then cut into beads.

Venetian glass is handmade in Italy and is sometimes called Murano glass. These beads are prized for their vivid colors and beautiful designs.

FINDINGS & STRINGING MATERIALS

Once you've selected your beads, you'll need some findings—all the odds and ends that come together to turn your beads into a piece of finished jewelry—as well as some beading wire, cord, or other fiber for stringing. Findings are usually made of metal, and that metal can be anything from gold to inexpensive, nonprecious base metal.

Headpins hold beads in place and can be used for embellishments and connections. Plain headpins look like a skinny nail; decorative headpins have a fancy end. You'll usually find these in lengths from 1–3 in. (2.5–7.6 cm), and you may have a choice of wire thickness. If the hole in your bead is too large for the end of the headpin and it slips right through, just string a seed bead or spacer first and you'll be all set. Eye pins have a loop at the end that holds the bead in place, can be linked to another loop, or acts as a decorative embellishment.

Sterling silver and gold-filled wire are often used for making fine jewelry. You may see other choices, including brass, steel, and copper. (Brass and copper wire from the hardware store are great practice materials—they are inexpensive and easy to manipulate!) The most common wire **profile** is round, although you may also encounter half-round, square, and twisted options. **Gauge** is the diameter (or thickness) of the wire; the larger the number, the thinner the wire. A good, all-purpose choice is 22 gauge. Thinner 26-gauge will pass through small holes, such as those in pearls. For projects such as bracelets, where you need a sturdy wire, you might choose thick 16 gauge. When buying precious-metal wire, you may have a choice of **hardness**. Half-hard wire is a good choice for most projects; choose dead-soft if you plan to do a lot of coiling or wrapping. As you hammer, bend, and shape metal, it gets firmer, or work-hardened. **Memory wire** is steel wire that has been formed into coils. It's strong and holds its shape. Use heavy-duty wire cutters to trim this wire (it will damage jewelry-grade cutters) or bend it back and forth until it breaks.

For stringing a **stretch-cord or elastic** bracelet, you can use a monofilament cord, such as Stretch Magic, or a flat, ribbon-like strand made of many filaments bonded together, such as Gossamer Floss. Monofilament cord is strong and easy to use, but knots may not hold. Ribbon elastic is easy to string onto if you use a beading needle, and the flat strand holds knots well. A bonus is that the multifilament ribbon elastic will fray before it breaks, giving you a chance to save and repair your jewelry. Whichever type you choose, it's always a good idea to glue your knots.

Jump rings are connectors. You'll find them in a range of diameters, sizes, finishes, and styles. Thicker gauges work well when the jump rings are part of the design. Jump rings are sold "open" (not soldered) or soldered shut. They can be round or oval in shape. **Split rings** are like tiny key chains; the spiral of wire keeps whatever you've attached—a link of chain, a dangle with a loop, a manufactured charm—in place. Another use for jump rings is linking them to create chain mail jewelry.

ESSENTIALS

Phew! That was a lot to cover. I wanted you to see all of your options for stringing materials and tools. But what do you really need to get started?

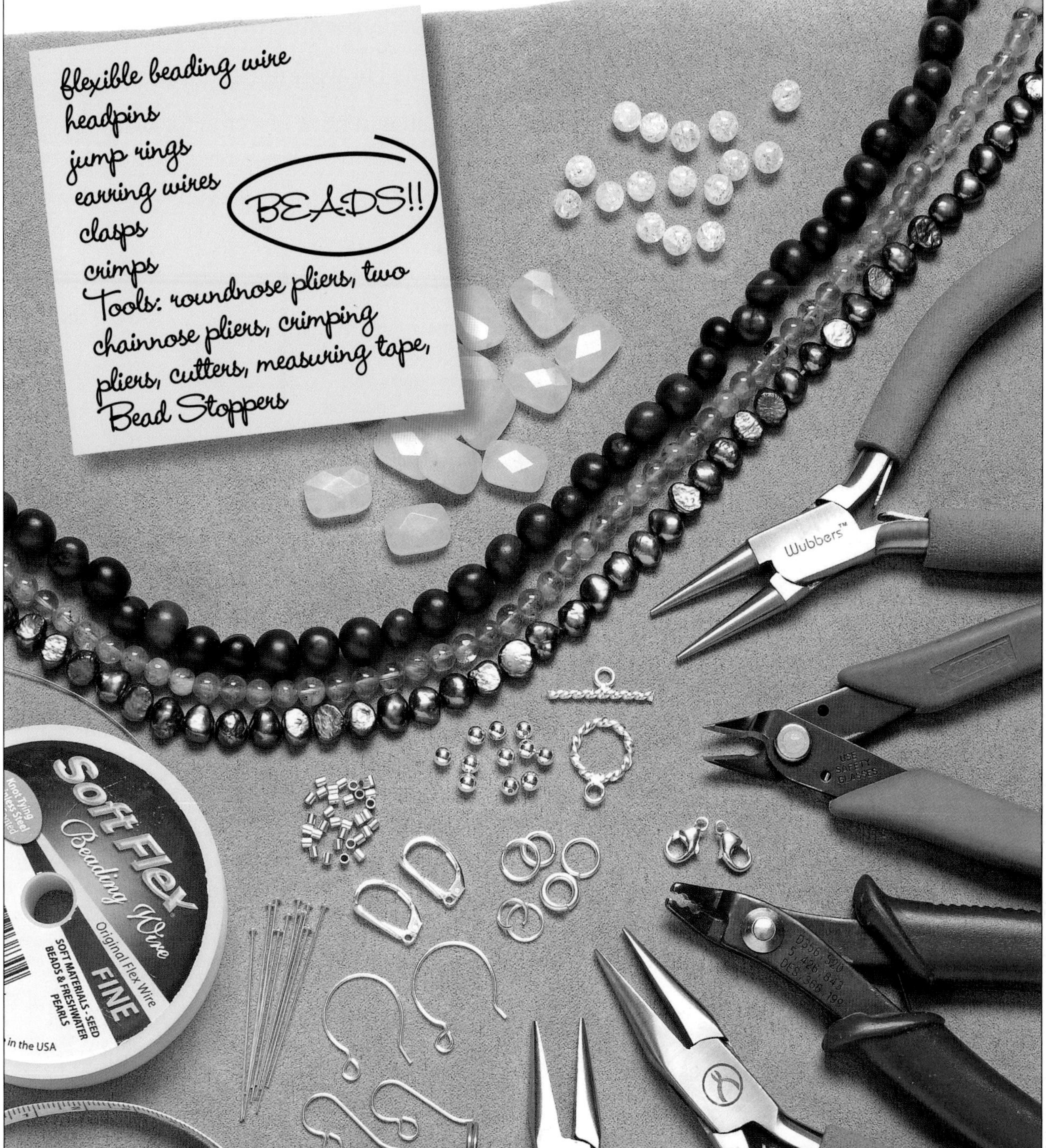

flexible beading wire
headpins
jump rings
earring wires
clasps
crimps
Tools: roundnose pliers, two chainnose pliers, crimping pliers, cutters, measuring tape, Bead Stoppers
BEADS!!
Wubbers™
USE SAFETY GLASSES
Soft Flex
Beading Wire
Original Flex Wire
FINE
SOFT MATERIALS - SEED BEADS & FRESHWATER PEARLS

WORKSPACE

You're back from the bead store, ready to go with your new stash of beads, your essential tools, and your necessary findings. Now what? Assuming you don't have a studio of your own (not many of us do), you'll have to claim a workspace. Because my studio is a corner of my dining room table, I need a functional space while I'm working and I need to be able to clean up quickly, too. Here are the key things I like to have near me for beading.

A **bead mat** made from nonlinty fabric is a nice, soft work surface that keeps beads from rolling around. Purchase bead mats at the craft or bead store, or use a kitchen towel set into a cookie sheet. (Bonus: I teach you how to make a beading work board on p. 90.)

Ah, vanity. No, the **mirror** isn't to check your hair and makeup—you'll need it to check the fit of your necklace before you make the final crimp. It's important to look at where your necklace falls and how it sits against your neck. You may check and adjust the fit several times before you finish.

A **bead board** has several channels that hold beads steady and a few wells to hold your working beads. It's marked with measurements so you can plan your work. I don't use one often, but for certain projects, it's a must-have.

A full-spectrum **task light** will save your eyes and show the details and true colors of your work. That's really important when you're trying to accent or match colors. It's amazing how artificial indoor lighting can change the appearance of certain colors.

STORAGE

There are probably as many storage systems as there are crafters. I started with divided bead boxes (see below right), but quickly acquired more beads than they could hold. I settled on a method I call "contained chaos." I have a **set of stacking trays** that are about two inches deep—one for gemstones and pearls, one for chain and wire, one for seed beads, and one for crystals. Although the trays keep things tidy, within the trays my strands and baggies sometimes get a little messy (thus the contained chaos). I spread them out when I'm working so I can see my materials at a glance. When I'm done, they stack up and tuck neatly away on a shelf.

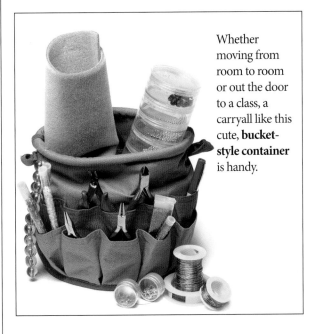

Whether moving from room to room or out the door to a class, a carryall like this cute, **bucket-style container** is handy.

I now use my **original divided boxes** for findings, like crimps, clasps, jump rings, and headpins.

As you move forward with your new hobby, your preferences will drive your storage and organization system. Do you like to choose by color? Or is it texture and material that matter to you? You may decide to organize by shape or size instead. It's likely that a solution will gradually present itself, and it will be perfect—just for you.

crimping
measuring

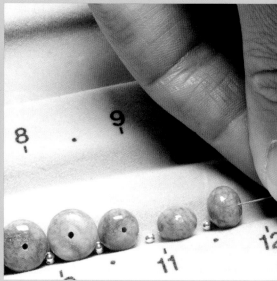

Stringing Projects

fitting

designing

PROJECT 1
Simple strung necklace

Finished length: 17 in. (43 cm)

MATERIALS

- 15- or 16-in. (38 or 41 cm) strand 6–8 mm faceted gemstones
- **4** 3 mm round beads
- **2** crimp tubes
- Toggle clasp
- Flexible beading wire, .014
- Chainnose pliers
- Diagonal wire cutters

TIP Bead sizes are always in millimeters. This is an industry standard, so when you're shopping for beads, that's the way you'll see them marked. After a while, you'll get used to thinking about 4 mm and 6 mm beads as an average size, and you'll recognize that 12 mm beads are pretty large.

These faceted gemstones are pretty enough to stand on their own. Buy a temporarily strung strand of beads, transfer them to flexible beading wire, and add a clasp.

ABSOLUTELY!

Gemstones

Gemstone beads are usually sold on strands. Sometimes the strands are knotted together, and a bead-store staffer will help you choose one to buy and cut it from the group for you. Strands are often 16 in. (41 cm) long, but you may notice variations of an inch or so. After you add your clasp, this length should be enough for a short necklace, especially if you add accent beads to the design. Some stores sell half strands, which is nice when you want to mix a variety of gemstones in a single necklace project.

1. Determine the finished length of your necklace, add 6 in. (15 cm), and cut a piece of beading wire to that length. The extra length gives you a little flexibility in adjusting the fit of the necklace, and it makes it easier to bring the ends back through the crimp tubes. When you have more experience, you can reduce the extra length by a few inches.

2. String a crimp tube, a spacer bead, and half the clasp on the wire.

TIP

Stringing a bead on each side of the crimp creates a buffer, so the sometimes-sharp edge of the crimp is less likely to fray the wire as the clasp is handled over time.

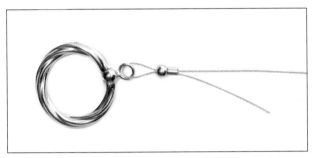

3. Bring the wire end back through the spacer bead and the crimp tube. Pull the wire through, creating a small loop.

4. Grasp the crimp with chainnose pliers and squeeze gently to flatten.

5. String a spacer bead over the working wire and the wire tail. Move the bead close to the flattened crimp. Trim the excess wire tail with wire cutters, being careful not to cut the working wire.

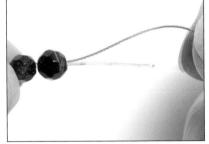

6. Transfer the strand of gemstones to the flexible beading wire. Hold the temporarily strung strand in your nondominant hand, and the beading wire in the other hand. Pass the beads from the strand onto the beading wire.

7. String a spacer bead, a crimp, a spacer bead, and the remaining clasp half. Bring the wire back through the beads just strung. Tighten the wire and check the fit. Remove beads to adjust the fit, if necessary. Use chainnose pliers to flatten the crimp. Trim the excess wire.

TIP

It may sound obvious, but the length of your necklace is limited to the length of your strand and the size of your clasp. You may have to purchase two strands of beads to reach your desired length. Use the extra beads to make a bracelet!

PROJECT 2

Pattern with two bead sizes

Finished length: 20 in. (51 cm)

MATERIALS

- 15- or 16-in. (38 or 41 cm) strand of 8 mm round gemstones
- **50–60** (less than 1 g) 11º seed beads
- **4** 3 mm spacer beads
- **2** crimp tubes
- 2-part hook clasp
- Flexible beading wire, .014
- Chainnose pliers
- Diagonal wire cutters

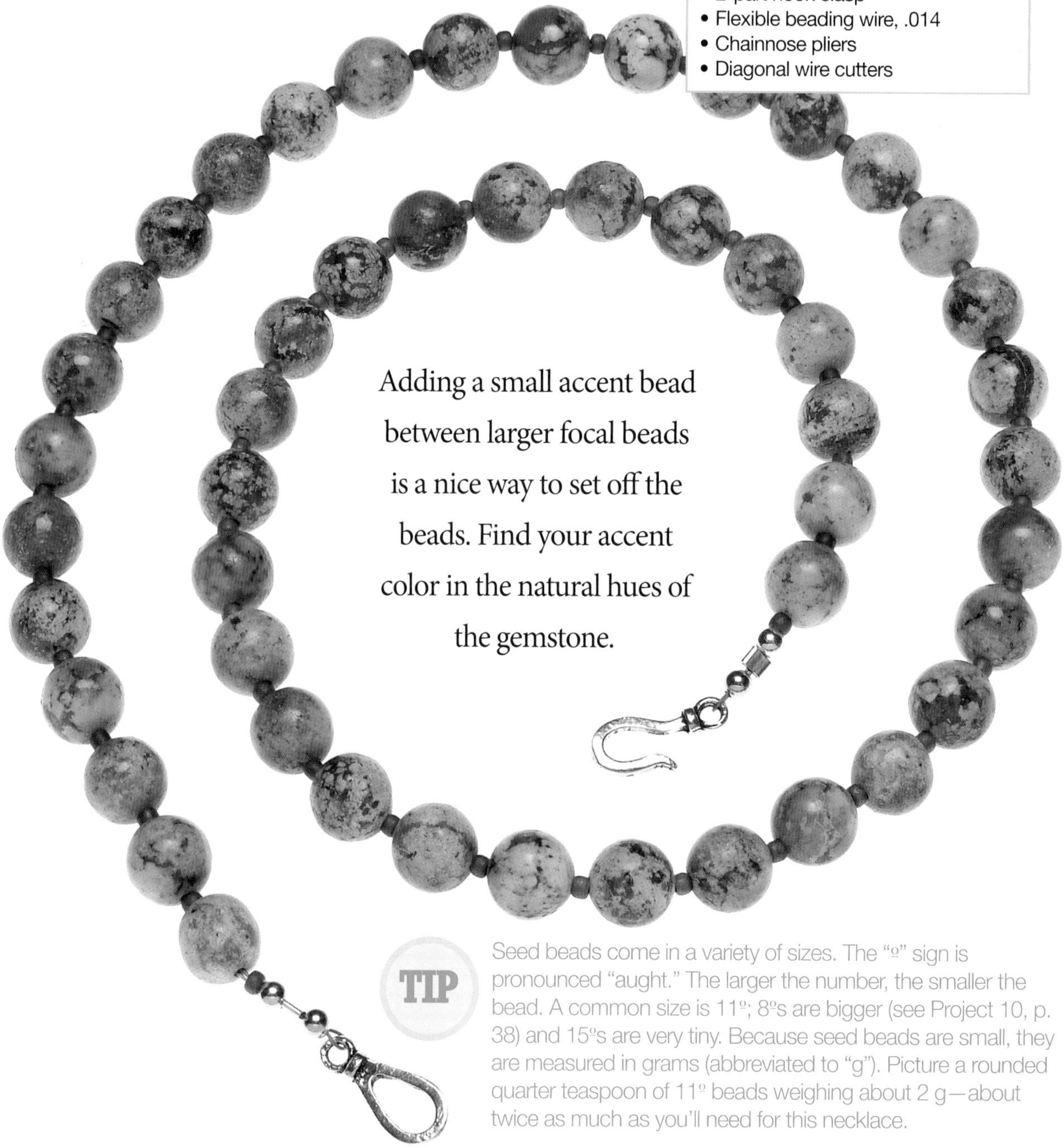

Adding a small accent bead between larger focal beads is a nice way to set off the beads. Find your accent color in the natural hues of the gemstone.

TIP

Seed beads come in a variety of sizes. The "º" sign is pronounced "aught." The larger the number, the smaller the bead. A common size is 11º; 8ºs are bigger (see Project 10, p. 38) and 15ºs are very tiny. Because seed beads are small, they are measured in grams (abbreviated to "g"). Picture a rounded quarter teaspoon of 11º beads weighing about 2 g—about twice as much as you'll need for this necklace.

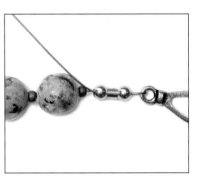

1. Determine the finished length of your necklace, add 6 in. (15 cm), and cut a piece of beading wire to that length. String a crimp tube, a spacer bead, and half the clasp. Bring the wire end back through the beads just strung, leave a short tail, and use chainnose pliers to flatten the crimp.

2. String a 3 mm round spacer bead, an 11º seed bead, and a gemstone. Alternate seed beads and gemstones until the necklace is about 1 in. (2.5 cm) shorter than the desired length. Cover the wire tail as you add beads.

3. String a 3 mm round, a crimp tube, a 3 mm round, and half the clasp. Go back through the beads just strung and tighten the wires. Check the fit and add or remove beads, if necessary. Take a moment to check your work and make sure the pattern is right (see Tip below). If all is well, use chainnose pliers to crimp the crimp tube. Use wire cutters to trim the excess wire.

TIP Check your work before you make the final crimp. If you find an extra seed bead, one option is to remove the beads from the wire, fix the mistake, and restring.

You also can gently break the seed bead with crimping pliers. Work over a wastebasket or a piece of paper, covering the pliers with your hand to keep shards of glass from flying. (Better yet: Wear safety glasses.) You can accommodate the slack by tightening the wire again. Mistake fixed; you're ready to finish the necklace!

ANOTHER IDEA

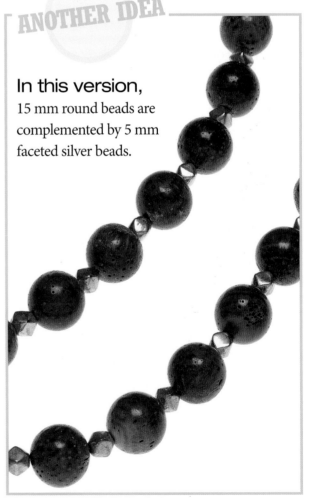

In this version,

15 mm round beads are complemented by 5 mm faceted silver beads.

PROJECT 3
Pattern with more differentiation

Finished length: 19 in. (48 cm)

MATERIALS

- **9** 20 mm disk beads, color A
- **8** 20 mm disk beads, color B
- **18** 3 or 4 mm gemstones
- **36** 3 mm flat spacers
- **2** 3 mm round beads
- **2** crimp tubes
- 2-part hook clasp
- Flexible beading wire, .014
- Crimping pliers
- Diagonal wire cutters

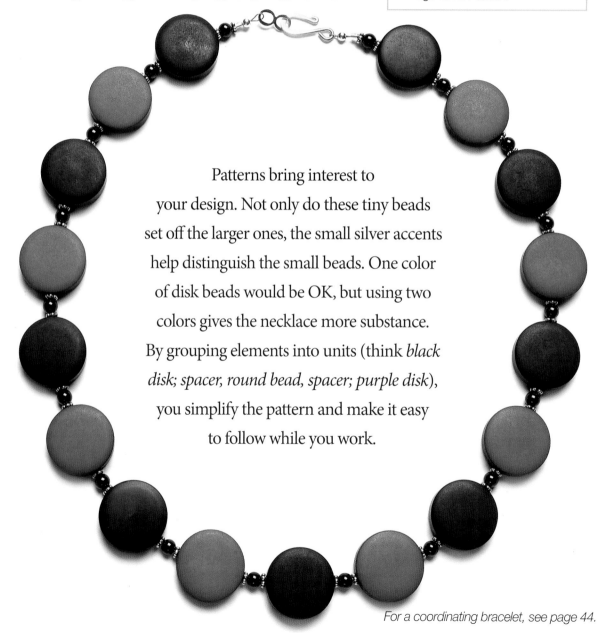

Patterns bring interest to your design. Not only do these tiny beads set off the larger ones, the small silver accents help distinguish the small beads. One color of disk beads would be OK, but using two colors gives the necklace more substance. By grouping elements into units (think *black disk; spacer, round bead, spacer; purple disk*), you simplify the pattern and make it easy to follow while you work.

For a coordinating bracelet, see page 44.

1. Cut a piece of beading wire 6 in. (15 cm) longer than the desired length of your necklace. String a crimp tube, a 3 mm round bead, and half the clasp. Bring the wire end back through the beads just strung and tighten the wire.

2. Place the crimp in the notch closest to the handles of the crimping pliers. Separate the wires as shown and squeeze the pliers.

3. Reposition the pliers so the crimp is positioned vertically in the notch closest to the tip of the pliers.

4. Gently squeeze the two sides together to make a folded crimp. As you add beads, string over both wires until the tail is covered.

5. String: 3 mm flat spacer, 4 mm gemstone, 3 mm flat spacer, color A disk, 3 mm flat spacer, 4 mm gemstone, 3 mm flat spacer, color B disk.

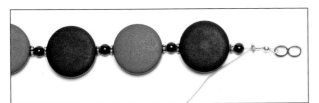

6. Repeat Step 5 until the necklace is within ½ in. (1.3 cm) of the desired length. Check your work to be sure the pattern is accurate. Make any necessary adjustments (I added another color A disk to end the necklace). String a 3 mm flat spacer, a 4 mm gemstone, a 3 mm flat spacer, a crimp, a 3 mm round bead, and half the clasp. Bring the wire end back through the beads just strung and tighten the wire. Check the fit of the necklace, and add or remove beads if necessary.

7. Make a folded crimp as you did in Steps 3 and 4. Trim the wire tail.

Beading wire

No matter how carefully you plan a design or how exotic the beads are, your finished jewelry is only as good as the material you string it on. Have you ever inherited a necklace and noticed that the stringing thread has stretched so much that the necklace has gaps? Or worse, have you found a jumble of a necklace with frayed or broken threads? Understanding the basics of stringing material will help you make good choices before you start and guarantee happiness long after you finish.

While it can look as thin as a thread, flexible beading wire is made of bundles of steel wire bound together and coated with clear nylon. It is strong, sturdy, and it doesn't stretch. Using flexible beading wire on a project today means it will hold its shape for years to come.

The diameter is how thin or thick the wire is: .012 is very thin; use it for lightweight beading projects. For most jewelry, .014 is an average diameter that works well. For large gemstone nuggets, heavy beads, or substantial pendants, choose .019.

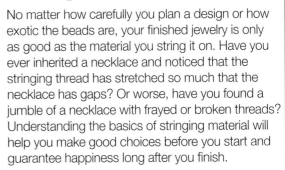

PROJECT**4**
Necklace of graduated beads

Finished length: 21 in. (53 cm)

MATERIALS

- 14–16-in. (36–41 cm) strand graduated beads
- **10** 4 mm round spacers
- **8** 3 mm round spacers
- **24–28** 2.5 mm round large-hole spacers
- **2** crimp tubes
- Clasp
- Flexible beading wire, .014
- Bead Stoppers (or tape)
- Crimping pliers
- Diagonal wire cutters
- Bead board

TIP

You don't *have* to use the beads in the exact order you find them. Exchange same-size beads if you prefer a different color placement, as I did with two yellow-veined beads. They were next to each other; I moved them to be opposite each other.

Graduated sizes keep these bold beads from becoming overwhelming when strung together. The spacer beads are a nice complement; they gradually decrease in size along with the gemstones. Having smaller beads at the back makes the necklace comfortable to wear.

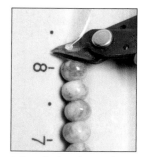

1. Lay the bead strand in a channel of the bead board. Cut the knot in the temporary string. Remove the string, leaving the beads in the same order.

TIP

You should have no problem passing wire through the large-hole 2.5 mm beads a second time.

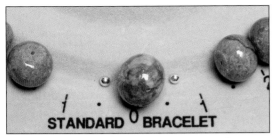

2. Beginning at the center, place a 4 mm round spacer on either side of the largest bead. Intersperse 4 mms with the next five beads on each side of the center bead.

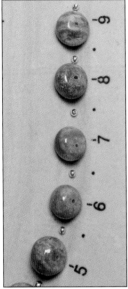

3. Place 3 mm rounds between the next five beads on each side.

4. Place 2.5 mm rounds between the remaining beads, ending with a round.

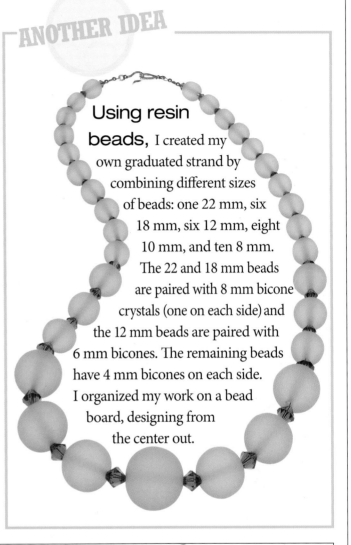

Using resin beads, I created my own graduated strand by combining different sizes of beads: one 22 mm, six 18 mm, six 12 mm, eight 10 mm, and ten 8 mm. The 22 and 18 mm beads are paired with 8 mm bicone crystals (one on each side) and the 12 mm beads are paired with 6 mm bicones. The remaining beads have 4 mm bicones on each side. I organized my work on a bead board, designing from the center out.

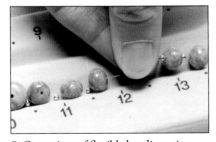

5. Cut a piece of flexible beading wire 6 in. (15 mm) longer than the measurement of the beads on the board. Place a Bead Stopper (or tape) on one end, and string the beads in order.

6. String a crimp tube, a 2.5 mm round, and half the clasp. Go back through the beads just strung and a few more, and tighten the wire.

7. Remove the stopper from the other end and repeat step 6. Check the fit, and add or remove an equal number of beads from each end if necessary. Make a folded crimp on each end and trim the wire.

PROJECT5
Center focus

Finished length: 19 in. (48 cm)

MATERIALS

- **3** 20 x 15 mm beads, silver
- 16-in. (41 cm) strand 6 mm round lava rock beads
- **4** 4 mm flat spacers
- **2** 4 mm round gemstones, black onyx
- **4** 3 mm round silver beads
- **2** crimp tubes
- Toggle clasp
- Flexible beading wire, .012
- Bead Stoppers
- Crimping pliers
- Diagonal wire cutters

When a focal design is centered, the necklace
needs to be built from the center out toward both
ends. It is much easier to adjust the fit (and keep
the design centered) if you can add or remove
beads from both ends.

1. Cut a piece of beading wire 6 in. (15 cm) longer than the desired length of your necklace. String a diamond, a flat spacer, a gemstone, a flat spacer, a diamond, a flat spacer, a gemstone, a flat spacer, and a diamond. Center the beads on the wire.

2. Place a Bead Stopper on one end of the wire.

3. On the other end, string about 7 in. (18 cm) of 6 mm round beads. Place a stopper on the wire.

4. Remove the stopper from Step 2, and string an equal number of round beads on this end. Replace the stopper. Check the fit of the necklace, allowing for the clasp. Add or remove an equal number of beads from each end if necessary.

5. On one end, string a 3 mm round, a crimp, a 3 mm round, and half the clasp. Go back through the beads just strung and a few more. Tighten the wire and make a folded crimp. Repeat on the other end with the remaining clasp half. Trim the excess wire.

TIP Since my beads had larger holes, I used .012 diameter beading wire, which is both sturdy and flexible. It's also good for heavier gemstones or metal beads.

ANOTHER IDEA

This polymer clay bead
is framed by warm white pearls, copper spacers, and crystals that pick up the blue of the flower in the clay bead. Copper-colored pearls complete the look.

PROJECT6
Center dangle

Finished length: 19 in. (48 cm)

MATERIALS

- Locket or pendant with a bail
- A few 11º seed beads
- 16-in. (41 cm) strand 8 x 5 mm oval gemstones
- 16-in. strand of 3 or 4 mm round gemstones
- **4** 6 mm rondelles or other accent beads
- **4** 3 mm round beads
- **2** crimp tubes
- Clasp
- Flexible beading wire, .014
- Diagonal wire cutters
- Crimping pliers

This project adds a few twists into the pattern—are you ready for a challenge? We've got a pendant, two sizes of gemstones, and some accent beads. By starting in the center, you can build the pattern on each side. The primary design of the necklace is completed by Step 4, leaving freedom in Step 5 to control the length. If you need to adjust the fit, just add or remove a few beads; you won't have to redo the focal pattern of the necklace you created in Steps 1–4.

TIP

A bail is the loop attached to a pendant that allows it to hang from the stringing material.

1. Cut a piece of beading wire 6 in. (15 cm) longer than the desired length of your necklace. String a few seed beads and the locket on the wire.

2. Center the beads on the wire so the seed beads tuck under the locket's bail. This gives the locket a resting place and keeps the gemstones you'll string next from traveling under the bail. On each end, string a round gemstone and an oval gemstone. Alternate shapes for a total of three round and two oval on each end.

3. On each end, string a rondelle, five round gemstones, and a rondelle.

4. String an alternating pattern of round and oval gemstones on each end, beginning and ending with a round, until the necklace is within 1 in. (2.5 cm) of your desired length.

5. Check the fit of the necklace, allowing for the clasp. Add or remove beads from each end if necessary. On one end, string a 3 mm round, a crimp, a 3 mm round, and half of the clasp. Go back through the beads just strung. Tighten the wire and make a folded crimp. Repeat on the other end with the remaining clasp half. Trim the excess wire.

TIP

Labradorite is a gray gemstone with flashes of yellow, green, or blue. This locket has a lustrous moonstone on the front. I chose marcasite accent beads because they sparkle and reflect the silverwork of the locket. I used a box clasp that features a labradorite in a setting; when closed, this style of clasp creates a very neat finish.

PROJECT7
Simple multistrand necklace and bracelet

The strands of this necklace are all the same length. Using double lengths of beading wire simplifies the beginning steps. You can easily modify the look by using fewer strands or smaller beads. Because this necklace doesn't have a center focal pendant, you'll work from one end to the other, adjusting the fit by adding or removing beads from just one end. The bracelet uses two pairs of wires instead of three, for a total of four strands. Assemble it in the same way as the necklace. I like to twist these a bit before clasping them.

Finished length: 17 in. (43 cm)

MATERIALS Necklace

- **400** fire-polish Czech glass rondelles, assorted colors
- **120** 4 mm bicone crystals, assorted colors
- **6** 3 mm round beads
- **6** crimp tubes
- Toggle clasp
- Bead Stoppers
- Flexible beading wire, .012
- Crimping pliers
- Diagonal wire cutters

Finished length: 7½ in. (19 cm)

MATERIALS Bracelet

- **2** 16-in. (41 cm) strands 4 mm Czech glass crystal beads, assorted colors
- **40–45** 3 mm bicone crystals, assorted colors
- **4** 3 mm spacer beads
- **4** crimp tubes
- Toggle clasp
- Bead Stoppers
- Crimping pliers
- Diagonal wire cutters

TIP

Bulky strands take up space, so check the fit carefully. On your neck, a multistrand 17-in. necklace may fit like a choker.

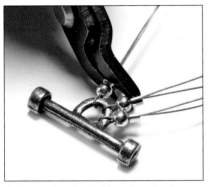

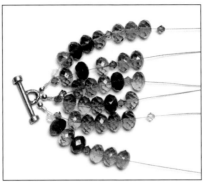

1. Determine the finished length of your necklace, add 3 in. (8 cm), and cut three strands of beading wire to double that length. String one wire through half the clasp and bring the ends together. String a round bead and a crimp tube over both ends. Position the beads near the clasp and make a folded crimp. Repeat with the two remaining wires.

2. Begin stringing beads and crystals on the wires. I like to work for a few inches on each wire, so I can watch where the colors are landing and keep a varied pattern throughout the necklace.

TIP Because you'll go back through the beads with two wire ends to attach the second half of the clasp, be sure to use a thin (.012) beading wire and a round bead with a large hole.

3. When the strands are beaded to your desired length (allowing for the clasp to be added), string a crimp and a round bead over each pair of wire ends. Place a Bead Stopper on the two outside pairs of wire ends. Bring the ends of the middle pair through the remaining clasp half and back through the beads. Tighten the wires and make a folded crimp. Trim the excess wire. Working with one pair of wire ends at a time, remove the stopper and finish as you did with the middle pair.

ANOTHER IDEA

You can create a **similar necklace** with pearls. For an odd number of strands, string each strand separately. Gather them together and string one bead, one crimp, one bead, and half the clasp over all three strands. Go back through the beads and crimp. Most 4 mm spacer beads can accommodate six strands of .014 beading wire.

PROJECT8

Graduated-length multistrand necklace

Finished length: 19 in. (48 cm)

MATERIALS

- **3–4** 16-in. (41 cm) strands of 3–6 mm gemstones or pearls, assorted shapes and colors
- **30** 4–5 mm beads, silver
- **12** 3 mm round beads, silver
- **6** crimp tubes
- Three-strand clasp
- Flexible beading wire
- Bead Stoppers
- Diagonal wire cutters
- Crimping pliers

A multistrand clasp helps control a design like this because it separates the strands. You may have to check and adjust the fit several times in Step 3. Not only are you measuring the overall length of the necklace, but you're also checking the varied lengths of the strands against each other.

TIP A bead board can help you organize your patterns before you string.

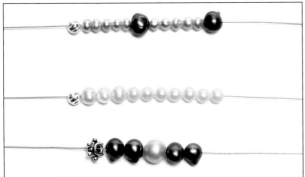

1. Determine the finished length of your longest strand. Add 6 in. (15 cm) and cut a piece of flexible beading wire to that length. Cut a second piece 1 in. (2.5 cm) shorter, and a third piece 2 in. (5 cm) shorter. My strands are 17, 18, and 19 in. (43, 46, and 48 cm). String a pattern of beads on the longest strand, using more of the larger pearls and gemstones. Repeat the pattern until the strand is close to the desired length. Place a Bead Stopper on each end. Repeat with the two remaining strands using smaller beads.

2. On one end of the longest strand, string a 3 mm bead, a crimp tube, a 3 mm, and an end loop of half the clasp. Go back through the beads just strung. Repeat on the other end. Repeat with the remaining strands, attaching the middle length to the center loop and the shortest length to the remaining outside loop.

TIP

Because the loops on the clasp are just ¼ in. (6 mm) apart, my necklace appears to have strands of equal lengths when I put it on. If you would like more distance between the strands, make your middle strand 2 in. (5 cm) longer than the shortest strand and the long strand 4 in. (10 cm) longer than the shortest.

3. Check the fit, and add or remove beads from both ends if necessary. Working with one strand at a time, make a folded crimp at each end. Trim the excess wires.

TIP If you find a strand isn't long enough in Step 3, a few extra spacers may be all you need.

PROJECT 9
Multistrand necklace with centered pendant

Finished length: 19 in. (48 cm)

MATERIALS

- Pendant with bail
- **3** 16-in. (41 cm) strands 4–6 mm pearls in assorted colors
- **1 g** 11º seed beads
- **2** 4 mm round beads
- **6** crimp tubes
- **2** cones
- Clasp
- 6 in. (15 cm) 20-gauge wire, sterling silver
- **2** 4 mm jump rings
- Flexible beading wire
- Chainnose pliers
- Roundnose pliers
- Diagonal wire cutters

Bringing several strands of a necklace together through cones provides a neat finish to the back and a somewhat casual look to the overall design. You'll learn how to make a wrapped loop out of wire that will gather the strands.

1. Determine the finished length of your longest strand, add 6 in. (15 cm), and cut a piece of beading wire to that length. Cut two more lengths of wire, one ½ in. (1.3 cm) shorter and one 1 in. (2.5 cm) shorter than the first. My finished strand lengths (including clasp) are 19, 18½, and 17½ in. (48, 47, and 45 cm). String a few seed beads and the pendant on the longest wire. Center the pendant over the seed beads.

2. String a pattern on both sides of the pendant until the necklace is within 1 in. (2.5 cm) of the desired length.

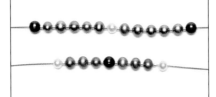

3. String a pattern on the remaining strands until they are within 1 in. of the desired length.

4. Cut 3 in. (7.6 cm) of wire, and make a wrapped loop at the end. (See Technique 2 on p. 91; follow the directions for making a wrapped loop with no bead, just wire.) Repeat this step and set the second loop aside.

5. On the longest wire, string a crimp tube and the loop. Come back through the crimp, add a few more beads, and tighten the wire. Repeat with the remaining strands, keeping them in order from longest to shortest.

6. Repeat Step 5 on the other ends of the wires, using the second loop from Step 4. Check the fit, estimating the additional length of the cones and the clasp. Be sure the strands hang the way you'd like. If necessary, adjust the fit by adding or removing beads from each end. Crimp the crimp tubes and trim the beading wire.

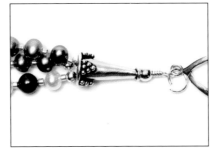

7. String a cone and a 4 mm bead on one wire. Slide the cone to cover the crimped ends and make a wrapped loop above the bead. Repeat on the other end. Attach one half of the clasp to each end with jump rings (see p. 92).

see p. 92

ANOTHER IDEA

A top-drilled gemstone

substitutes for a pendant in this version. The rough-cut tourmaline nuggets are balanced by smooth glass pearls and small gemstone beads. The strands are 19, 17, and 16 in. (48, 43, and 41 cm) long. The strand with the pendant is the longest, which makes this necklace very easy to wear.

PROJECT 10
Short asymmetrical necklace

Finished length: 19 in. (48 cm)

MATERIALS

- 6-in. (15 cm) strand resin nuggets, pink
- 6-in. strand resin nuggets, brown
- **1 g** 8° seed beads, pink
- **1 g** 8° seed beads, brown
- 10 in. (25 cm) open-link chain
- 5 mm jump ring
- Toggle clasp
- **2** crimp tubes
- Flexible beading wire, .012 or .014
- **2 pair** chainnose pliers
- Crimping pliers
- Diagonal wire cutters

By their very nature, asymmetrical necklaces are jaunty and a little whimsical. The bold resin beads would have been overwhelming on their own; the open chain adds a sense of airiness and is a perfect foil to the chunky nuggets. The floral clasp completes the presentation.

TIP

Some resin beads like these have large holes. If the hole is larger than the seed-bead spacers, just string enough seed beads to go through the resin beads.

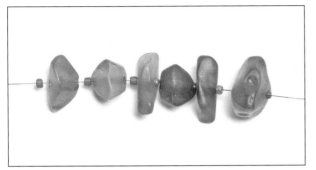

1. Determine the finished length of your necklace. Cut the chain to half this length. Cut a 15-in. (38 cm) length of wire. Alternate pink nuggets with brown seed beads and brown nuggets with pink seed beads and over the wire, ending with a seed bead, until the beaded portion is equal to half the desired length.

2. String a crimp tube, a seed bead, and an end link of chain. Come back through the beads just strung. Make a folded crimp.

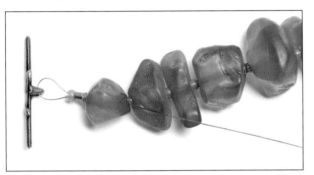

3. On the other end, string a crimp, a seed bead, and half the clasp. Tighten the wire, but do not crimp the crimp tube.

4. Attach the remaining clasp half to the other chain end with a jump ring. Check the fit, and adjust if necessary by trimming the chain. Make a folded crimp. Trim the excess wire.

TIP Wear the necklace with the clasp to the side or to the back.

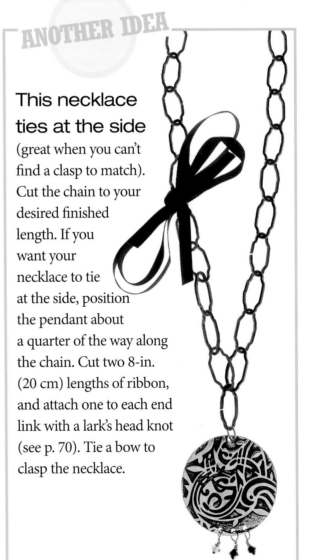

ANOTHER IDEA

This necklace ties at the side

(great when you can't find a clasp to match). Cut the chain to your desired finished length. If you want your necklace to tie at the side, position the pendant about a quarter of the way along the chain. Cut two 8-in. (20 cm) lengths of ribbon, and attach one to each end link with a lark's head knot (see p. 70). Tie a bow to clasp the necklace.

PROJECT 11
Long asymmetrical necklace

Finished length: 38 in. (1 m)

MATERIALS

- 3–12 mm gemstones in a variety of colors and shapes
- 5–7 mm silver accent beads
- 3–5 mm silver spacers
- 6⁰ seed beads
- 11⁰ seed beads
- **2** crimp tubes
- **2** crimp covers (optional)
- Clasp (optional)
- Flexible beading wire, .018 or .019
- Crimping pliers
- Diagonal wire cutters
- Chainnose pliers (optional)

While it's easy to say "anything goes" when it comes to a necklace like this, keep a few things in mind to make for smooth stringing. Plan the placement of your major elements (in my necklace, the gemstone beads). Find some smaller beads to balance the look and then use seed beads to space things out. When you're planning the length, consider whether you'd ever wear this doubled into two strands. If so, make the final length double what you're comfortable with for a shorter strand.

Off-center doesn't mean unbalanced. There are blue beads on the left and again on the right. The colors repeat and play off each other throughout the necklace.

1. Gather your materials together. Choose beads with similar finishes, but in different colors and shapes. Choose larger beads to accent your necklace and smaller beads for spacers. Determine the finished length of your necklace.

2. Plan your necklace. Use a design board or arrange the beads on your work surface. Start with the largest beads and fill in with smaller beads later on. When you're comfortable with your design, cut a piece of flexible beading wire about 3 in. (7.6 cm) longer than your desired length, and string the beads.

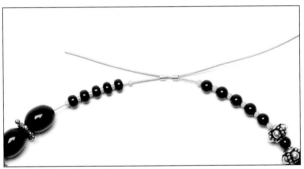

3. When you've reached your desired length, string two crimp tubes. Pass the tail end of the wire through both crimps in the opposite direction and pull the wires tight.

4. Fold the crimps. Cover with crimp covers, if desired.

TIP

5. If you'd like to have the option of wrapping the necklace into a few shorter strands, string a clasp to make it easier to put on and take off.

I use repeats of three and five in necklaces like this; it helps me keep track of each pattern, and the odd numbers create pleasing asymmetry.

TIP

To exaggerate the asymmetry, I placed a single large silver bead toward the bottom but not centered.

PROJECT 12
Bead soup bracelet

This bracelet blends order (patterns) with a little disorder (changing bead sizes and patterns from strand to strand). The clasp helps keep each strand tidy, and the pattern mixing keeps it fun. Lapis can be expensive, so mixing 3 mm with 8 mm helps control costs.

Finished length: 8 in. (20 cm)

MATERIALS

- **20–25** 8 mm round gemstones
- **45–50** 4 mm round gemstones
- **25–30** 3 mm round gemstones
- **10–15** 3 mm beads
- **1–3 g** 11º seed beads or 1 mm silver spacer beads
- **6** crimp tubes
- 3-strand slide clasp
- Flexible beading wire, .012
- Crimping pliers
- Diagonal wire cutters

1. Determine the finished length of your bracelet, add 5 in. (13 cm), and cut three strands of beading wire to that length. String a pattern of beads on each strand. Use all the beads on all the strands, but choose more large beads for one, more small beads for another, and a mix of beads for the third.

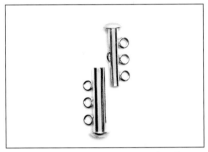

2. A slide clasp has loops on each side and slides together to close. I think it's easiest to work with the clasp in the closed position, to avoid twisting strands.

3. When the strands are close to your desired length, string a 3 mm bead, a crimp tube, a 3 mm bead and one loop of the clasp. Begin with the strand with the largest beads and the center loop of the clasp. Come back through the beads just strung and tighten the wire.

4. Repeat Step 3 with the remaining strands, and repeat with all three strands on the other side. Before crimping the crimp tubes, check the fit. Add or remove beads from each end, if necessary.

5. Make folded crimps. It helps to start with the center strand. Trim the excess wires.

TIP

Big beads take up more space on your wrist. To get a perfect fit, you may find that your big-bead strand needs to be a little longer than your other strands. That's why it's so important to check the fit in Step 4 before you crimp.

PROJECT13
Stretch-cord bracelet

A bracelet strung on ribbon elastic is easy to make and comfortable to wear. The continuous loop creates an endless pattern.

Finished length: 8¼ in. (21 cm)

MATERIALS

- **4** 20 mm disk beads, color A
- **4** 20 mm disk beads, color B
- **8** 3 or 4 mm gemstones
- **16** 3 mm flat spacers
- Ribbon elastic
- Twisted-wire beading needle
- Scissors
- Clear tape
- G-S Hypo Cement
- Flexible measuring tape

TIP For the pattern to work perfectly, this bracelet ended up a little larger than I would normally wear. (If I took out two disk beads, it would be too small. If I took out one disk bead, I'd have two of the same color next to each other). I could have alternated the disks with just one gemstone, doubled the small pattern, or used a single color of disks to come closer to the fit I wanted. You may need to experiment to get the fit you like.

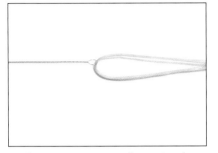

1. Measure your wrist to determine the finished length of your bracelet. Add 3 in. (7.6 cm), double the length, and cut a piece of ribbon elastic to that length. Center a twisted-wire beading needle on the elastic, and tape the ends together.

2. String: 3 mm flat spacer, 4 mm gemstone, 3 mm flat spacer, color A disk, 3 mm flat spacer, 4 mm gemstone, 3 mm flat spacer, color B disk. Repeat until the bracelet is the desired length.

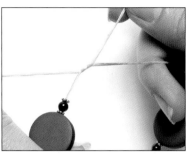

3. Cut the needle from the elastic and remove the tape from the other end. Tie a surgeon's knot with both strands: First, cross left over right and go through.

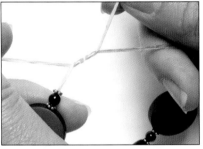

4. Go through again. Pull the ends until the knot is positioned next to the beads.

5. Cross right over left and go through once. Pull the knot tight.

6. Dab some glue on the knot.

7. When the glue is dry, trim the ends, and gently slide the knot into a bead.

Stretch-cord basics

ABSOLUTELY!

A popular and durable choice in stretch cord for beading is a brand called Stretch Magic. Because the cord is round, it's easy to string beads on the end. I've found that it's hard to tie knots in a round cord, though, because the knots tend to slip (gluing the knots helps).

Another kind of stretch cord is ribbon elastic such as Gossamer Floss, which is what I used in this bracelet. This elastic is very stretchy and flat, like dental-floss tape. It's easy to string beads if you use a twisted-wire beading needle, and the flat cord holds a knot well. (It's always a good idea to glue your knots, even when you're using ribbon elastic.)

Doubling the elastic doubles your chances of saving your work if the elastic breaks or a knot comes loose.

PROJECT 14
Multistrand stretch-cord bracelet

Experiment with color as you string this bracelet. Choose single colors for some strands or mix hues all the way through. An easy route is to buy multicolored hanks and string the beads they way they come off the thread. If you're a planner, choose tubes of complementary colors and enjoy plotting a design. Loops that are studded with pretty and functional crimp covers pull it all together.

Finished length: 7½ in. (19 cm)

MATERIALS

- Hank of 8⁰ seed beads or 5 g each of 4 colors
- **5** crimp tubes
- **5** crimp covers
- Flexible beading wire, .012
- Ribbon elastic
- G-S Hypo cement
- Twisted-wire beading needle
- Chainnose pliers
- Crimping pliers
- Diagonal wire cutters
- Scissors
- Tape

To open a crimp cover, slide it onto the tip of your round-nose pliers and gently push it against the jaw.

1. Determine the finished length of your bracelet, add 3 in. (8 cm), and cut a piece of ribbon elastic to double that length. Center a beading needle on the elastic, and tape the ends. String beads until the beaded portion equals the desired length.

2. Cut the needle from the elastic and remove the tape from the ends. Tie a surgeon's knot. Dab glue on the knot.

3. Repeat Steps 1–2 nine times for a total of 10 bracelets. Make sure all of the glue is dry and trim the elastic ends as close to the knots as you can. If the bead holes are large enough, gently slide each knot into a bead.

4. Cut a 4-in. (10 cm) length of beading wire. String 28 seed beads and a crimp tube.

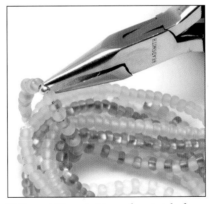

6. Tighten and make a folded crimp. Trim the wire ends.

7. Repeat Steps 4–6 to make a total of five loops. Position a crimp cover over a folded crimp and use chainnose pliers to squeeze it shut. Repeat with the remaining crimps.

5. Pass the wire through the set of 10 bracelets, and bring the wire tail through the crimp.

TIP Twisted-wire beading needles have a collapsible eye so they can go through small beads. When you're done working with one, use the tip of a straight pin to gently reshape the eye so you can thread more elastic and use it again.

chain

jump rings

wire loops

dangles & charms

Connecting
Projects

PROJECT 15
Easy chain bracelet

Copper jump rings are inexpensive and easy to maneuver because the metal is soft—qualities that make them perfect for practicing. Using two pairs of chainnose pliers gives you the best control, but you can also use a pair of chainnose and a pair of roundnose. After you're comfortable with opening and closing copper rings, try sterling silver. You'll find it a bit harder to move, but you'll get used to it quickly.

Finished length: 7½ in. (19.1 cm)

MATERIALS

- **54–66** 5 mm jump rings, copper
- Clasp
- **2** pairs of chainnose pliers

TIP

You don't have to open and close all of your jump rings in Steps 2 and 3. Just make a little pile of open rings and another pile of closed rings. When you get tired of opening and closing, begin to assemble the bracelet. When you're out of rings, take a break from assembling to restock the piles.

1. To open a jump ring, hold chainnose pliers in a parallel position on each side of the jump ring's opening.

2. Gently push one pair of pliers forward and one toward you, keeping them straight. The jump ring will open. Open about 27 jump rings.

3. To close a jump ring, hold the pliers in the same position as step two, but bring them in the opposite direction, back to the center. You will feel the two sides of the ring meet in the middle, as if they've clicked together. Check the join with your finger to be sure you've made a smooth connection. Close about 27 jump rings.

 TIP Don't be afraid to move the ends of the jump ring back and forth a few times in Step 3 to get them to meet perfectly.

4. Use an open ring to pick up three closed rings. Close the open ring.

5. Pick up the single ring with an open ring, and close the ring. Repeat once.

6. Use an open ring to pick up three closed rings, and also the end single ring from Step 5. Close the ring. Pull three rings forward so you have three grouped rings, three single rings, and three grouped rings.

7. Repeat Steps 4–6 until the bracelet is within ½ in. (1.3 cm) of your desired length. End with three single rings. Attach three single rings to the other end as well.

8. Open the last jump ring and attach half the clasp. Repeat on the other side.

ANOTHER IDEA

This version uses larger rings with a heavier gauge. Combining sets of two and three give this bracelet weight and impact.

PROJECT 16
Wrapped-loop earrings

Forming wrapped loops is an important skill to master, because they bring an increased dimension to your bead stringing. Wrapped loops are secure connections that open the door to making beaded earrings and dangles. Dangles let you progress from the horizontal line of strung beads to add a vertical element. Let's practice with earrings and move on from there.

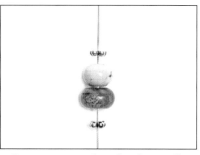

1. String a spacer, a large bead, a small bead, and a spacer on a headpin.

2. Grasp the headpin above the spacer with chainnose pliers. Bend the wire over the pliers to make a right angle.

3. Position the roundnose pliers in the bend as shown.

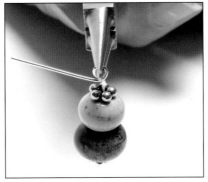

4. Bend the wire up and over the top jaw.

5. Reposition the roundnose pliers so the lower jaw is snug in the partial loop—this tells you that you're working at the same place on the jaw. Bend the wire around the lower jaw to complete the loop.

 TIP At the end of Step 5, you've made the first half of the wrapped loop. At this point, you can slide the loop onto a piece of chain, an earring finding, or attach it to another loop. Once you complete the wraps in Step 6, you have a permanent and secure connection.

ANOTHER IDEA

Silver squares are bracketed

by flat spacers and completed with wrapped loops for stylish and secure dangles.

6. Grasp the loop with chainnose pliers, and use roundnose pliers or your fingers to wrap the tail around the stem until the tail is snug to the bead.

7. Trim the end with wire cutters.

9. Open the loop on an earring wire and attach the dangle. Close the loop.

10. Make a second earring to match the first.

TIP

Diagonal wire cutters leave an angled cut that tucks in neatly next to the wraps. Try using the single curved notch in your crimping pliers to guide the wire end.

8. Gently squeeze the cut end with chainnose pliers to tighten the wraps.

PROJECT 17
Chain necklace with dangles

Finished length: 18 in. (46 cm)

MATERIALS

- 12–16 in. (30–41 cm) chain (I used 5.25 mm oval link)
- **5–7** 10 mm oval beads
- **4–6** 5 mm round beads, silver
- **9–13** decorative headpins
- **2** 5 mm jump rings
- Lobster claw clasp
- Chainnose pliers
- Roundnose pliers
- Diagonal wire cutters
- Crimping pliers

Enhance an open chain with a few wrapped-loop dangles and add a clasp, and you have an instant necklace. Make a few extra dangles for matching earrings.

1. String a bead on a headpin and make the first half of a wrapped loop above the bead. Repeat with all oval and round beads.

2. Determine the finished length of your necklace and cut the chain to that length. Find the center link of chain by holding the two end links together. The center link will dangle in the middle. If you have two links in the middle, cut a link from one end of the chain.

3. Attach an oval bead to the center link of chain and complete the wraps.

4. Attach a round bead unit on each side of the oval bead and complete the wraps. Repeat, alternating oval beads and round beads until all the units are attached.

5. Open a jump ring, string the end link of chain and the clasp, and close the jump ring. Attach a jump ring to the other end of the chain.

ANOTHER IDEA

Smooth gemstones and rough pearls provide a light and airy look.

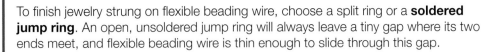

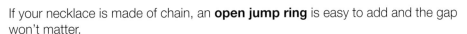

TIP

Lay your chain on a flat surface and be sure that your links are straight. Connect each loop to the same side of the chain. You'll have to straighten out the chain after you make each connection.

ABSOLUTELY!

All about rings

To finish jewelry strung on flexible beading wire, choose a split ring or a **soldered jump ring**. An open, unsoldered jump ring will always leave a tiny gap where its two ends meet, and flexible beading wire is thin enough to slide through this gap.

If your necklace is made of chain, an **open jump ring** is easy to add and the gap won't matter.

A **split ring** can be manipulated on or off (just like a key ring), but you shouldn't need to take it off once it's on. Split rings can look bulky, so consider the overall design of your piece before choosing one.

The gap of an **oval jump ring** hangs at the side instead of the top, so gravity makes it less likely that beading wire will slide through. Oval jump rings are a good substitute for soldered or split rings. If you're attaching a charm or a pendant to the front of a necklace strung on wire, an oval jump ring is a good choice. It's more streamlined than a split ring and the gap is less likely to matter than that of a round jump ring.

PROJECT18
Dangle earrings

With earrings like these, they're the only accessory you need. Make them as full as you like. These are 2 in. (5 cm) long, but if you prefer a more subtle look, shorter is fine. Use the best quality crystals—even tiny 3 mm clear crystals will flash in the light from across the room.

MATERIALS

- **2** 8 mm cube crystals
- **4** 6 mm bicone crystals
- **14–18** 4 mm bicone crystals
- **8–12** 3 mm bicone crystals, assorted colors
- **8–12** 3–6 mm pearls, assorted shapes and colors
- 4 in. (10 cm) long-and-short chain
- **2** 1½-in. (3.8 cm) decorative headpins
- **34–46** 1 in. (2.5 cm) headpins
- **2** 3 mm jump rings (optional)
- **2** lever-back earring wires
- Chainnose pliers
- Roundnose pliers
- Diagonal wire cutters

TIP

I find it easier to build these earrings together, alternating from one chain to the other to keep things balanced. I prefer a mirror-image look to these earrings, so I attach components to opposite sides of each chain. You'll see what I mean as soon as you start adding beads.

1. Cut the chain into two 2-in. (5 cm) pieces, leaving a short link on each end.

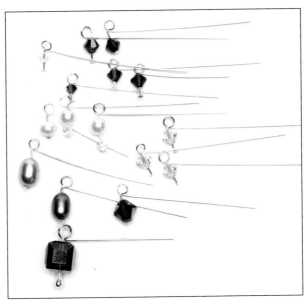

2. Gather your beads, string one or two on a headpin, and make the first half of a wrapped loop above the bead. Use decorative headpins for the 8 mm cubes and plain headpins for the rest. Make dangles in matching pairs, and reserve one for each earring.

3. Attach a cube dangle to an end link of chain and complete the wraps. Repeat with the second 8 mm cube on the second chain segment.

4. Attach a 6 mm bicone crystal dangle to a chain link. Attach the second 6 mm crystal dangle to the other chain, on the opposite side of the link. Complete the wraps. Working from the bottom up, attach dangles to each side of each chain. Complete the wraps.

5. When the earrings are as full as you'd like, open the loop of an earring wire (or use a jump ring) and attach the top link of chain. Close the earring wire or jump ring. Repeat with the second earring.

ANOTHER IDEA

Use similar pearls but change the crystals to shades of green to create a new look.

PROJECT19
Plain-loop earrings

Making plain loops is another key skill to master. These simple loops provide a subtle connection. Although they make excellent links, they can be pulled open, so they are best used for lightweight components or jewelry that won't see a lot of wear and tear.

MATERIALS

- **2** 12 mm round beads
- **2** 10 mm round beads
- **4** 1½ in. (3.8 cm) 20-gauge headpins
- Pair of earring wires
- Chainnose pliers
- Roundnose pliers
- Diagonal wire cutters

TIP

If you don't want to pull out the ruler in Step 2, place a 10 mm bead on top of the first bead and trim the wire directly above the second bead. Remove the bead. The wire will be the perfect length for making the loop.

1. String a 12 mm round bead on a headpin. If the hole is larger than the head of the pin, string a seed bead or flat spacer first.

2. Trim the wire ⅜ in. (1 cm) above the bead. Use your fingers to make a right-angle bend in the wire directly above the bead.

3. Use roundnose pliers to grip the tip of the wire. Use your fingertip to check that the tip doesn't extend past the other side of the jaws.

4. Rotate your wrist to roll the wire around the lower jaw until you can't rotate comfortably any more.

5. Remove the pliers from the loop. Insert the lower jaw into the loop you've just made until it's snug to ensure that you're working at the same place on the jaw. Rotate your wrist again, rolling the pliers to complete the circle.

6. Trim the end from a headpin. Make a right-angle bend ⅜ in. (1 cm) from the end. Repeat Steps 3–5 to make a plain loop at the end of the wire. String an 8 mm round bead above the loop, and repeat Steps 2–5 to make a plain loop above the bead.

7. Open the loop at the bottom of the 8 mm bead unit and connect it to the 12 mm bead unit. Close the loop.

8. Open the loop on an earring wire and connect the dangle. Close the loop. Make a second earring to match the first.

ANOTHER IDEA

Create a variety of looks
with your new skill!

TIP Using wrapped loops instead of plain loops would extend the length of these earrings and show a lot more silver between the beads. Use wrapped loops when a secure connection is important; use plain loops to showcase the beads.

Troubleshooting

Extra wire? Your working tail was too long. Gently trim the excess wire close to the original bend.

Not enough? Your working tail was too short. It's best to start over with a new length of wire, and perhaps work closer to the tips of the roundnose pliers.

Oval loop? Double-check the placement of your pliers in Step 5. If you didn't slide the loop back to your starting place, you'll lose the roundness of the loop. Marking your pliers with a permanent marker can help you find your place.

PROJECT20
Dangle pendant with earrings

A little elegant or a little eclectic? Control the look of this bold necklace with your choice of elements. I like larger beads with open-link chain, but you can easily re-create this on a much smaller scale and maintain the impact.

Finished length: 28 in. (71 cm)

MATERIALS

- **3** 10–20 mm gemstone nuggets
- 12 mm gemstone briolette
- **3** 8–10 mm silver beads
- **2–3** 3–5 mm silver flat spacers
- **5** 2-in. (5 cm) plain or decorative headpins
- 3 in. (7.6 cm) wire, 20–22-gauge
- 12 mm jump ring, 16-gauge
- **2** 5 mm jump rings
- 26 in. (61–66 cm) 8–10 mm link chain
- Lobster-claw clasp
- Chainnose pliers
- Roundnose pliers
- Diagonal wire cutters

1. Trim the end from a headpin and string a briolette on the wire. Position the bead so it is slightly off center. Make a right angle bend on each side of the bead.

2. Cross the wires above the bead to form a triangle shape.

3. Use chainnose pliers to bend each wire at the intersection so they form a right angle.

4. Position chainnose pliers across the triangle and hold the unit. Use a second set of pliers to wrap the short end of wire around the stem. Make a wrapped loop above the wraps to complete the dangle.

TIP Briolettes often have small holes. You may need a 24- or 26-gauge headpin to fit through the hole.

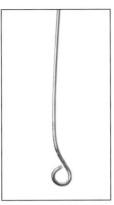

5. Make a small loop at one end of the 3-in. (7.6 cm) wire.

6. String two nuggets on the wire. Make a wrapped loop above the top bead.

7. Create additional dangles by stringing a spacer and a bead on a headpin and making a wrapped loop above the beads.

8. Open a 12 mm jump ring and string on the dangles, placing the largest dangle in the center.

9. Find the center link of the chain and string it on the jump ring. Close the jump ring.

10. Use a 5 mm jump ring to attach a lobster-claw clasp to one end of the chain. Attach a 5 mm jump ring to the other end of the chain.

Earrings to complement

1. String a flat spacer and round bead on a headpin and make a wrapped loop above the bead.

2. Make a set of wraps above the briolette. Make a wrapped loop above the wraps.

3. Open a 5 mm jump ring and string a teardrop bead. Close the jump ring.

4. Open a 10 mm jump ring and string a bead dangle, a briolette dangle, and a teardrop dangle. Close the jump ring.

5. Open an earring wire and string a dangle. Close the earring wire. Make a second earring to match the first.

MATERIALS

- **2** 12 mm gemstone briolettes
- **2** 6 mm round silver beads
- **2** 8 mm silver beads, teardrop shape
- **2** 5 mm flat spacers
- **4** 2-in. (5 cm) headpins
- **2** 5 mm round or oval jump rings
- **2** 10 mm 16-gauge jump rings
- Pair of earring wires

PROJECT 21
Cluster bracelet

Finished length: 8 in. (20 cm)

MATERIALS

- **3** 6-in. (15 cm) strands glass chips
- **32–40** dagger beads
- **8–10** rectangle spacer beads
- **5–10** silver charms
- **38–40** 2-in. (5 cm) headpins
- **35–45** 5 mm jump rings
- Chain bracelet or 7½ in. (19.1 cm) chain and clasp
- **2** pairs of chainnose pliers
- Roundnose pliers
- Diagonal wire cutters

Make this bracelet out of almost anything. String beads into wrapped-loop dangles, and use jump rings to attach charms. I like to make these bracelets as full as possible, but a more subtle approach works equally well.

TIP

To make a pre-made bracelet smaller, remove the ring end of the clasp, trim a few links of chain, and replace the ring. To make the bracelet adjustable, move the ring about 1 in. (2.5 cm) from the end link (keep this portion free of beads), and add a dangle to the last loop for decoration.

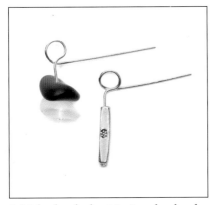

1. Make dangles by stringing glass beads on a headpin and making the first half of a wrapped loop above the beads. Make at least one glass-bead dangle for every link of chain. Make silver dangles by stringing a rectangle bead on a headpin and making the first half of a wrapped loop above the bead. Make 8–10 silver dangles.

2. Open a jump ring and string a glass dagger. Make a dagger charm for every link of chain. Make charm dangles by opening a jump ring, stringing a charm, and closing the jump ring. Make 5–10 charm dangles.

3. Working from the center of the chain, attach a glass-bead dangle to one side of a link and complete the wraps. Attach a dagger charm to the other side of the link and complete the wraps. Continue attaching dangles and charms, changing sides as you go, until you've attached one of each to each link.

4. Place silver bead dangles, as desired, along the length of the bracelet and complete the wraps.

5. Attach silver charms along the bracelet as desired.

6. Make a beaded dangle by stringing three dagger beads onto a jump ring. Link it to the last link of the bracelet and close the jump ring.

ANOTHER IDEA

Sometimes less
is more. This version has just one bead per link.

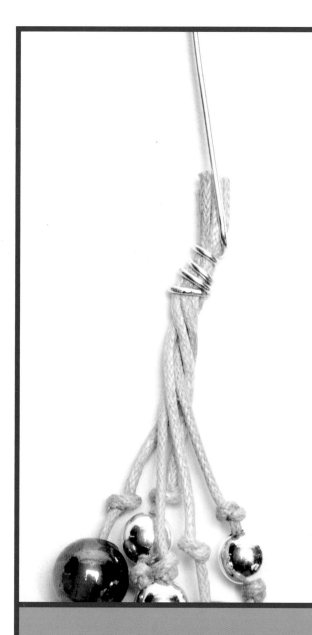

Fiber Fun

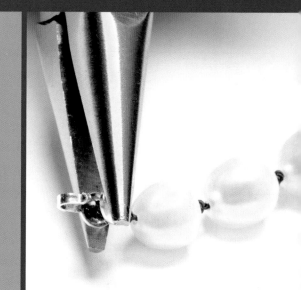

knotting

finishing cord ends

PROJECT 22
Knotting pearls

Finished length: 19 in. (48 cm)

MATERIALS

- 16-in. (41 cm) strand of pearls
- No. 3 silk cord with attached needle
- **2** bead tips
- **2** 3 mm jump rings
- Pearl clasp
- Awl or needle
- Chainnose pliers
- Scissors
- G-S Hypo Cement

In this casual interpretation of the classic pearl necklace, you'll string all the pearls onto the cord before you begin tying knots. The knots prevent the pearls from rubbing against each other and keep the entire strand from tumbling should the cord break. Years ago, pearls were quite precious, but today you'll be able to find freshwater pearls that are quite affordable yet beautiful.

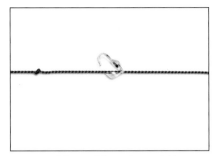

1. Unwind the cord from the card. Tie an overhand knot about 6 in. (15 cm) from the end opposite the attached needle. String a bead tip with the opening facing the knot.

2. Slide the bead tip to cover the knot. Make a second overhand knot but do not tighten it.

3. Use an awl or needle to slide the knot close to the bead tip. String all the pearls onto the cord, keeping them toward the end opposite the bead tip.

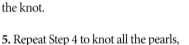

4. Slide a pearl next to the knot. Tie an overhand knot, using the awl to slide the knot next to the pearl before you tighten the knot.

5. Repeat Step 4 to knot all the pearls, checking the length as you go.

6. String a bead tip and slide it snug to the last knot. Tie an overhand knot. Tie a second knot for security. Position the knots inside the bead tip and dab with glue. Finish the other end with a second knot and glue in the same way. When the glue is dry, trim the cord ends. Use chainnose pliers to close the bead tips.

7. Connect the bead tip loop and half of the clasp with a jump ring. Gently squeeze the bead tip loop closed. Repeat on the other end with the remaining clasp half.

Design note: This oval clasp is sometimes called a fish-hook clasp, although you may see them sold as "pearl clasps." Because it takes two steps to fasten—you hook the loop and then slide the hook into the clasp—it's very secure. It's traditional for pearls, because they can be quite valuable and the two-step mechanism acts as a safety if the necklace becomes unclasped.

TIP

Keep box clasps and slide clasps closed when you attach them to the necklace so you don't accidentally reverse one half of the clasp.

PROJECT23
Knotting a big-bead necklace

Finished length: 21 in. (53 cm)

MATERIALS

- 16-in. (41 cm) strand 15 mm round gemstone beads
- 1 yd. (.9 m) 1 mm waxed cotton cord
- 12 in. (5 cm) 24-gauge wire, copper
- Lobster-claw clasp
- 2 links of chain
- Bead Stopper
- Awl or needle
- Chainnose pliers
- Scissors

The only difference between this necklace and the knotted pearl necklace on p. 66 is that the larger beads call for thicker cord. This necklace makes an attractive choker and it's also striking when made longer. For a super-long look, you'll need a second strand of beads.

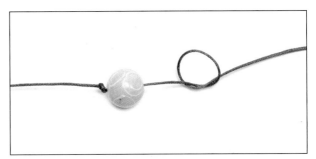

1. Tie an overhand knot at one end of the cord, leaving a 2-in. (5 cm) tail. String all the gemstones onto the cord and secure the end with a stopper. Slide all but one bead away from the knotted end.

2. Slide the bead next to the knot. Tie an overhand knot on the other side of the bead.

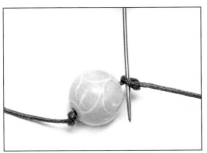

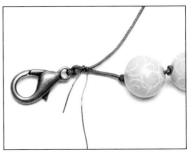

3. Use the awl or needle to slide the knot next to the bead.

4. Repeat Steps 2–3 to make a knot between all the beads, checking the length as you go.

5. String the clasp onto the cord, and knot the clasp in place ⅜ in. (1 cm) from the last knot.

6. Trim the cord end to ¼ in. (6 mm). Using half the wire, bind the cord end in place.

7. Repeat Steps 5–6 on the other end, substituting the chain links for the clasp.

TIP Big beads are heavy, and your cord may stretch over time. Be careful to knot the strand as tightly as you can.

TIP Use leftover chain links as a clasp loop. I used two links from a long-and-short link chain and knotted the necklace to the smaller link. The lobster claw hooks into the large link .

PROJECT 24
Simple pendant on silk ribbon

Finished length: 21 in. (53 cm)

MATERIALS

- 40–70 mm gemstone donut
- **2** strands silk ribbon
- **2** fold-over crimp ends
- **2** jump rings
- S-hook clasp
- G-S Hypo Cement
- Chainnose pliers
- Scissors

On one of my first outings to the bead store, I bought a few of these gorgeous donuts. I got home and was all set to make a necklace—until I realized I couldn't figure out a way to string a donut and have it lie flat. I didn't know what a bail was, let alone how to make one. After I learned how easy it is to tie a lark's head knot, I use this handy connection in all kinds of jewelry.

1. Determine the finished length of your necklace. Cut the silk strands 2 in. (5 cm) longer than that length.

2. Make a lark's head knot: Hold the strands together and fold in half. Bring the fold through the gemstone donut. Pass the ends of the strands through the loop. Pull the ends to secure the knot. Double check the length, trimming the ends if necessary.

3. On one end of the necklace, apply glue to the very ends of the silk and fold the raw edges over. Position the folded end in the crimp end.

4. With chainnose pliers, gently squeeze one side of the crimp end shut.

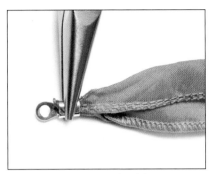

5. Squeeze the other side of the crimp end over the first.

6. With cutters, trim any stray fibers.

7. Repeat Steps 3–6 on the other necklace end.

8. Open a jump ring, and attach half of the clasp to the crimp end. Close the jump ring. Repeat on the other end with the remaining clasp half.

ANOTHER IDEA

Rather have a bail?
String seed beads and a crimp bead on a piece of flexible beading wire (as you did for the bracelet on p. 46). Bring the beaded strand through the donut, cross and tighten the ends in the crimp, and make a folded crimp. Finish the necklace as desired.

Suede lacing
is a natural complement to an organic turquoise pendant.

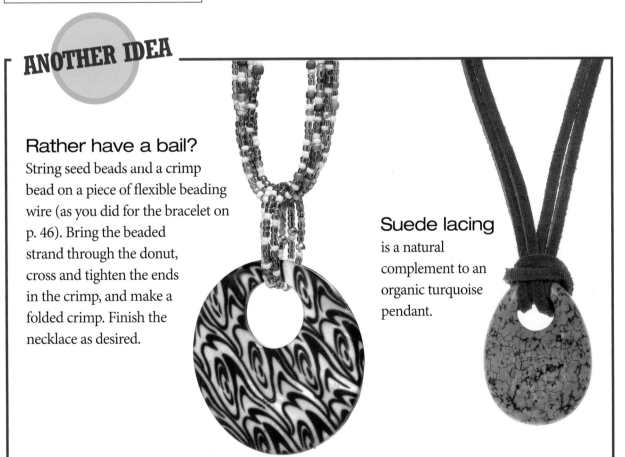

PROJECT25
Suede cord plus chain with dangles

I love using mixed materials in jewelry. The metal is hard and the suede is oh-so-soft. The copper is warm and the navy blue is rich. This necklace seems contemporary, but it would be equally at home with a classic outfit.

Finished length: 16 in. (41 cm)

MATERIALS

- **3** 10 mm round beads
- **8** glass chip beads
- **3** 1½-in. (3.8 cm) decorative headpins
- **4** 1-in. (2.5 cm) plain headpins
- **8** in. (20 cm) textured chain
- **1** yd. (.9 m) 3 mm suede cord
- **6** in. (15 cm) 22-gauge wire
- **2** fold-over crimp ends
- **2** 5 mm jump rings
- Clasp
- G-S Hypo cement
- Chainnose pliers
- Roundnose pliers
- Diagonal wire cutters

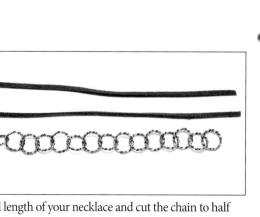

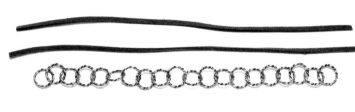

1. Determine the finished length of your necklace and cut the chain to half that length. Cut two pieces of suede cord, each equal to the chain length.

2. Make a chip-bead dangle: String a chip on a plain headpin and make the first half of a wrapped loop above the bead. Make four dangles. Make a round-bead dangle: String a round bead on a decorative headpin and make the first half of a wrapped loop above the bead. Make three dangles.

6. Bring the cord ends together and check the fit of the necklace, allowing for the clasp. Trim the cord if necessary. On one end, dab the cord ends with glue and place them in the fold-over crimp. With chainnose pliers, fold and gently squeeze one side of the crimp to the center. Repeat with the other side of the crimp.

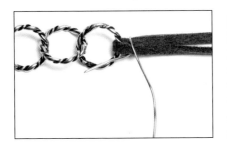

3. Find the center link of chain and attach a round-bead dangle. Complete the wraps.

4. On each side, attach a chip-bead dangle and complete the wraps. Be careful to work at the same place on each link; for my chain, it was at the bottom. Attach the remaining dangles, alternating rounds and chips.

7. Repeat Step 6 on the other end of the necklace.

8. Use a jump ring to attach half of the clasp to a crimp end. Repeat on the other end.

9. Using half the wire, make a right-angle bend about ¼ in. (6 mm) from the end. Place the wire in the folded cord end, near the chain link. Make four or five wraps around the folded cord, keeping the wraps close together. Trim the wire ends and tuck close to the wraps. Repeat on the other end.

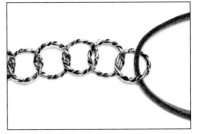

5. On one end, string a piece of cord through the last link. Repeat on the other end.

ANOTHER IDEA

Earrings are easy.

Make two extra dangles in Step 2 and attach to earring wires.

PROJECT26
Beaded leather cord

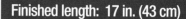

Finished length: 17 in. (43 cm)

MATERIALS

- **2** 12 mm large-hole beads, color A
- **3** 12 mm large-hole beads, color B
- **6** 8 mm glass rings
- **12** 8 mm large-hole flat spacers
- 18 in. (36 cm) 2 mm leather cord
- **2** crimp ends
- **2** 5 mm jump rings
- S-clasp
- G-S Hypo Cement
- Chainnose pliers
- Diagonal wire cutters

Less is more when you let your focal beads speak for themselves; a simple cord to display these beauties is all you need. Finish round cord off neatly with crimp ends that pinch the cord to hold it.

1. Determine the finished length of your necklace, subtract the size of the clasp, and cut the leather cord to that length. String: color A bead, flat spacer, ring, flat spacer, color B bead, flat spacer, ring, flat spacer, color A bead.

2. On each end, string: flat spacer, ring, spacer, color B bead, spacer, ring, spacer.

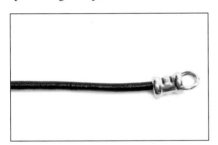

3. Dab a cord end with glue and place it in the crimp end. Repeat on the other end.

4. With chainnose pliers, squeeze the crimp in the center. Repeat on the other end. Let the glue dry.

5. Open a jump ring, and attach the crimp end and the S-clasp. Close the jump ring. Attach a jump ring to the other crimp end.

TIP Check that the crimp end you choose will accommodate your cord—crimp ends are available in different diameters.

TIP S-clasps are usually sold with both ends closed. Use chainnose pliers to gently open one tip of the S to create the hook side.

PROJECT27
Multistrand cord necklace

Knotting beads on cord creates a light, airy necklace. Allow some breathing room between beads to let the focal beads stand out. Sleek cones tame all the loose ends into a tidy finish.

Finished length: 22 in. (56 cm)

MATERIALS

- **3** 10 mm silver-lined glass beads
- **20–25** 6 mm round beads, silver
- **15–20** 6–8 mm round beads, glass
- 4 yd. (3.7 m) 1 mm cord, color A
- 3 yd. (2.7 m) 1 mm cord, color B
- 12 in. (30 cm) 20-gauge wire
- **2** 1-in. (2.5 cm) cones
- Lobster-claw clasp
- Chainnose pliers
- Roundnose pliers
- Diagonal wire cutters
- Awl or large needle
- Drinking straw
- Scissors

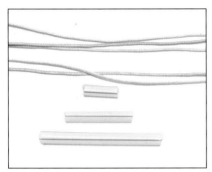

1. Determine the finished length of your necklace, and cut five pieces of cord to twice that length. Cut the straw into lengths of 2 in., 1 in., and ½ in. (5, 2.5, and 1.3 cm). Cut a lengthwise slit in each straw.

2. Center a silver-lined bead over all five cords. Make an overhand knot in all five cords on each side (use an awl or needle to guide the knot into place if necessary).

3. Using the largest straw as a guide, make another knot about 2 in. (5 cm) from the bead. String a silver-lined bead next to the knot and make a knot next to the bead. Repeat on the other side of the first bead.

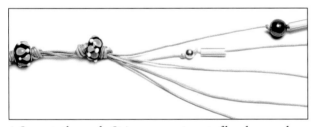

4. Separate the cords. String an assortment of beads on each cord, knotting on each side of each bead. Use the straws as a guide or space the beads randomly. Work from the center on both ends and check the fit as you go until you've reached your desired length.

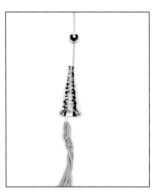

5. On one end, gather the cords together. Using half the wire, wrap about ½ in. (1.3 cm) of the cord end and leave a long wire tail. Trim the cord ends.

6. String the cone onto the wire tail. String a 6 mm bead.

TIP

The drinking-straw method is a little fussy (perfectionists may love it!). If it's not your thing and you're fine with slightly random spacing, abandon the straws and just eyeball the distance between the beads.

7. Make a wrapped loop above the bead. Use a jump ring to connect the loop with the clasp.

8. Repeat Steps 5–7 on the other end.

PROJECT 28
Wire mesh necklace

Finished length: 16 in. (41 cm)

MATERIALS

- **16–24** 8 mm faceted round Czech crystal beads
- **8** lampworked rings
- **8** lampworked drops
- 3 g 11º seed beads in two or more colors
- 48 in. (1.2 m) 6 mm tubular mesh
- 24 in. (61 cm) 2.5 mm tubular mesh
- 2 in. (5 cm) chain
- Flexible beading wire, .012
- **2** pinch ends
- **2** 5 mm jump rings
- Lobster-claw clasp
- G-S Hypo Cement
- Chainnose pliers
- Diagonal wire cutters

Wire mesh is fine-gauge wire woven into a mesh fabric. It's very soft against the skin and comfortable for necklaces and bracelets. It looks like a flat lace when it comes out of the box; with some gentle manipulation, you can achieve fantastic ruffles and flourishes. A short extender chain makes the length adjustable.

1. Cut two lengths of 6 mm mesh, one length of 2.5 mm mesh, and a piece of flexible beading wire 1½ times the desired length of your necklace. To string beads onto the mesh, twist one end to create a point.

2. String the faceted round beads on the 2.5 mm mesh. String an alternating pattern of a lampworked ring and a drop on each of the 6 mm lengths.

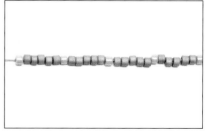

3. String a pattern of 25–30 seed beads on the flexible beading wire.

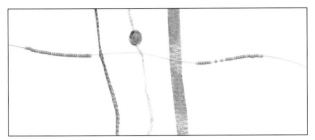

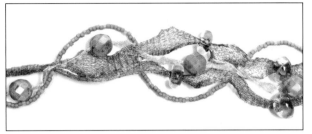

4. Bring the ends of the mesh together, and thread the beading wire through all three pieces about 2 in. (5 cm) from the end. If this is difficult at first, stretch the mesh to create a hole. Slide a round bead down to the beading wire. String another pattern of 25–30 seed beads on the wire.

5. Bring the end back through the mesh about 1 in. (2.5 cm) from the first stitch. You'll trap the round bead between the beading cord stitches.

6. String 25–30 seed beads, slide a round bead down as in Step 4, and come back through the mesh from the other side to create a wave pattern with the beaded wire.

7. Slide a ring down each 6 mm strand and a round bead down the 2.5 mm strand. String 25–30 seed beads, and bring the beading wire through the mesh again, trapping the beads as before. Repeat until all the lampworked beads have been used.

8. Repeat Steps 3–5.

9. Check the fit and trim the mesh ends. Weave the beading wire end through the mesh ends several times.

10. Pinch the mesh ends together and dab with glue. Place the mesh ends and the beading wire end in the pinch end. Use chainnose pliers to gently close the pinch end over the wires.

11. When the glue is dry, gently stretch and shape the wire mesh as desired.

12. Use a jump ring to attach the clasp to one pinch end.

13. On the other end, use a jump ring to attach the chain. Attach a wrapped-loop bead dangle to the chain end.

ANOTHER IDEA

Wire mesh gives you a lot of options for making quick-and-easy earrings.

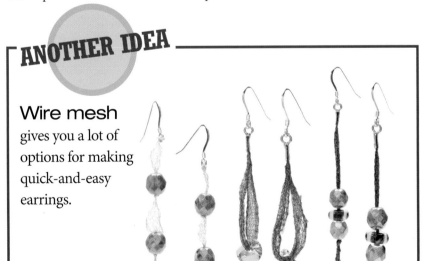

TIP

This necklace will stretch over time. After you've worn it, gently reshape the mesh as you did in Step 11.

PROJECT29
Two easy adjustable closures

Sometimes tracking down the perfect clasp is enough work to keep you from making the project! Knowing how to make these two knotted closures is a good skill to have in your bag of beading tricks. I like how these clasps become part of the jewelry piece.

Easy knotted necklace closure

1. String your necklace on cord as desired. Make sure the length of cord will pass over your head when joined. String a large-hole bead at one end.

2. Pass the other end through the bead in the opposite direction.

3. String a bead on the end of the cord and tie an overhand knot. Repeat on the other end.

4. Adjust the necklace by pulling on the ends.

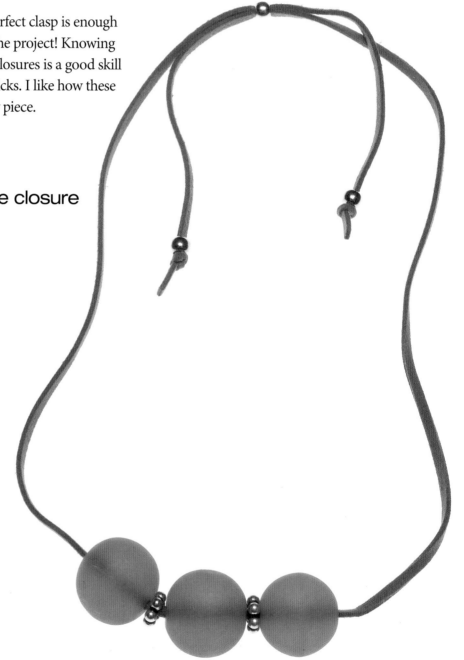

Bracelet slide closure using square knots

1. String your bracelet as desired over a single or double strand of cord. Using a drinking glass or other cylindrical object as a base, loosely drape the bracelet and tape the ends.

2. Cut a 1-yd. (.9 m) length of cord. Center the cord underneath the bracelet cords.

3. Make a square knot (see p. 93) around the bracelet cords.

4. Repeat Step 3 until the knotted section is about 2 in. (5 cm) long.

5. Tuck the ends under the knots and trim. Dab the ends with glue.

6. String a bead on a bracelet cord and tie an overhand knot at the end. Repeat with the remaining cords.

earring wires

extenders

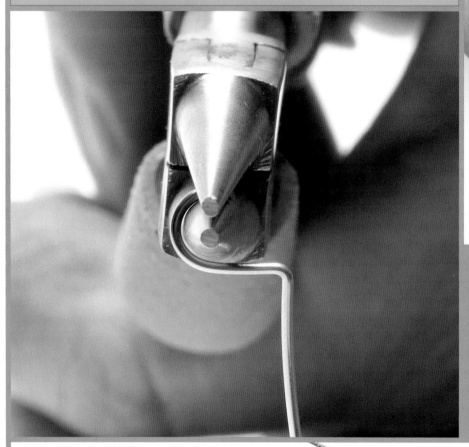

clasps

Extra Goodies

headpins

work board

PROJECT 30
Chain extender with dangle

MATERIALS

- 2–3 in. (5–7 cm) cable chain
- 6 mm bicone crystal
- **2** 3 mm bicone crystals
- 2 in. (5 cm) headpin
- Chainnose pliers
- Roundnose pliers
- Diagonal wire cutters

If you'd like to wear your necklace with different necklines, or if you're making a gift and you're not sure of the recipient's measurements, you'll likely want an adjustable fit. Here's a pretty and practical solution: Just substitute this extender for a soldered jump ring or split ring in any project that uses a lobster-claw or spring-style clasp.

String a 3 mm crystal, a 6 mm crystal, and a 3 mm crystal on a headpin. Make the first half of a wrapped loop above the top bead. Connect the dangle to one end of the chain and complete the wraps. Trim any excess wire.

PROJECT31
Toggle closure extender

MATERIALS

- Toggle clasp
- 3 in. (7.6 cm) cable chain
- **2** jump rings
- Chainnose pliers

I like the lengths of my favorite jewelry to shift with the seasons. In summer, I prefer my necklaces to fall within the neckline of my T-shirts. In the winter, I like them a little longer to lie around a turtleneck. A chain extender provides flexibility for lobster- or spring-style clasps. But what about a toggle closure? Here's a great solution.

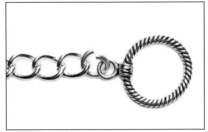

1. Open a jump ring. Attach half of the clasp to one end of the chain and close the jump ring. Repeat on the other end with the remaining clasp half.

2. To wear, insert the bar end of the extender in the loop end of the necklace, and the bar end of the necklace in the loop end of the extender. You've added 3 in. (7.6 cm) to the necklace—enough to comfortably fit around a turtleneck.

TIP

This extender matches the "Center Focus" necklace, p. 28.

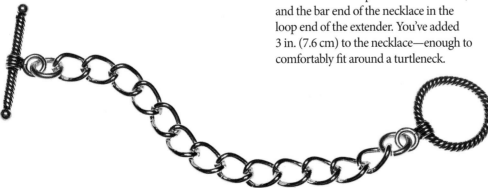

PROJECT 32
Headpins from wire scraps

Any wire scraps an inch or longer are worth saving. Here are two easy way to turn scraps into headpins.

Flat-end headpin for earrings

1. Hold the tip of the wire against the bench block. Strike the end of the wire with the flat face of the hammer to form a paddle shape. Turn the wire over and repeat on the other side.

Flat-end headpin

MATERIALS

- 1–2-in. (2.5–5 cm) wire scraps, 22-gauge or thicker
- Ball peen hammer
- Bench block

2. Test-fit a bead on the wire to make sure it can't slip past the paddle end.

Spiral-end headpin for a pendant

1. Working at the tip of your roundnose pliers, make a tiny loop at the end of the wire.

MATERIALS

- 4-in. (10 cm) length of wire
- Roundnose pliers
- Chainnose pliers

2. Use chainnose pliers to hold the loop, and use your fingers to bend the wire end into a spiral.

3. With chainnose pliers, grasp the wire at the top of the spiral and make a right-angle bend.

PROJECT33
Simple earring wires

Using just a few tools and short lengths of wire, it's easy to shape your own hook earring wires. Experiment with different round objects to result in a variety of shapes.

Version 1

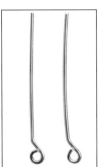

1. Cut two 2-in. (5 cm) lengths of wire and make a plain loop at one end of each wire.

2. Using roundnose pliers, grasp both wires about 1 in. (2.5 cm) above the loops, placing the wires at the widest point on the pliers' nose.

3. With your fingers, push the wires around the nose, creating a U-shaped bend.

4. Grasp both wires with the tip of the chainnose pliers and make a slight bend. Smooth the wire ends with the emery board.

Version 2

Follow Step 1 above, then grasp the wires together and curve them over a permanent marker or dowel, creating a wider curve than in Version 1. Bend the tips of both wires with chainnose pliers as in Step 4 above. Smooth the wire ends.

Version 3

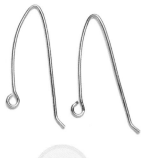

TIP

Shaping both earring wires together will help you get a perfect pair.

1. Follow Step 1 above using two 3-in. (7.6 cm) lengths of wire, then create a gentle curve above the loops by bending both wires around a film canister or prescription bottle.

2. Using chainnose pliers, grasp both wires above the curve and make a sharp bend. Bend the tips of both wires with the pliers as in Step 4 above. Smooth the wire ends.

PROJECT34
Clasp assortment

When supplies run short, it's handy to know how to make an easy beaded loop or shape clasps from wire. You may find that making your own closures becomes a creative extension of making your own jewelry.

MATERIALS

- 12 mm round bead
- 1 g 11° seed beads
- **2** crimp tubes
- Crimping pliers
- Diagonal wire cutters

Button-and-loop clasp

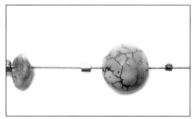

1. On one end of a beaded strand, string a crimp tube, a 12 mm round bead, and an 11° seed bead.

2. Skip the seed bead and go back through the round bead and the crimp.

3. Tighten the wire, crimp the crimp tube, and trim the excess wire.

4. On the other end, string a crimp tube and enough seed beads to make a loop that will fit snugly around the round bead.

5. Bring the tail back through the crimp, check the fit of the loop, and adjust if necessary. Crimp the crimp tube and trim the excess wire.

S-clasp

MATERIALS

- 2½ in. (6.4 cm) 18- or 20-gauge wire
- Roundnose pliers
- Diagonal wire cutters
- 4–6 mm bead (optional)

1. Cut a 2½-in. (6.4 cm) length of wire. Turn a small loop at one end.

2. Grasp the base of the loop near the base of the roundnose pliers' jaws.

3. Bend the wire around the jaw in the opposite direction of the loop.

4. Slide a bead on the wire.

5. Repeat Step 2, placing the pliers near the bend. Bend the wire in the opposite direction of the first bend to make an S shape.

6. Turn another small loop at the opposite end of the wire and going in the opposite direction.

7. Slide the bead to the middle. Gently hammer the two curved ends on both sides of the wire. To use, hook into a jump ring at each end of a necklace.

Hook-and-eye clasp

MATERIALS

- 6 in. (15 cm) 18- or 20-gauge wire
- Diagonal wire cutters
- Ball-peen hammer
- Bench block
- Roundnose pliers
- Chainnose pliers
- 4 mm round bead (optional)

1. Cut a 3-in. (7.6 cm) length of wire. Make the hook as in Steps 1–3 of the S-clasp. Working near the base of the jaw of your roundnose pliers, make a large wrapped loop at the opposite end of the wire.

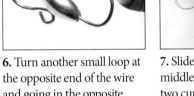

2. Cut a 3-in. (7.6 cm) length of wire. Make a large wrapped loop at one end.

3. Gently hammer the hook and eye shapes to strengthen and flatten the wire.

4. To attach to a necklace, make the first half of a wrapped loop at the other end of the eye wire and attach it to chain. Or finish the wraps and crimp a beaded strand to the loop.

PROJECT**35**
Beading work board

The ideal beading surface is smooth, lint free, and has a little give so it's easy to pick up beads with a needle or wire end. (It's so much easier to push the wire into the bead than it is to hold the bead in your fingers and try to string it onto the wire.) There are many commercial bead boards available. I've used everything from a dishcloth to a fabric remnant on a rimmed cookie sheet, but here I present my perfect combination.

MATERIALS

- ¼-in. (6 cm) plywood, 12 x 16 in. (30 x 41 cm)
- Quilt batting
- Fine microfiber fabric such as Ultrasuede
- Staple gun and staples
- Scissors
- Measuring tape

- Because most of my necklaces are 16 in. (41 cm) long, I can judge the length by the edge of the board as I work. Another idea is to glue a flexible measuring tape to the edge.
- The plywood is stiff enough to lift and move when it's time to clean up the work space. Do be careful of beads rolling off the edges.
- The fabric is a soft, lint-free surface. Its neutral color makes it easy to see most beads and findings. Note that felt is a poor choice—fibers will catch on beading wire ends.

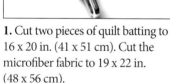

1. Cut two pieces of quilt batting to 16 x 20 in. (41 x 51 cm). Cut the microfiber fabric to 19 x 22 in. (48 x 56 cm).

2. Center the batting on the fabric and the board on the batting. Starting in the middle of one side, fold the fabric and batting toward the center. Staple. Repeat to secure each side.

3. Carefully staple the fabric at intervals of 1 in. (2.5 cm), being sure to keep the fabric smooth and even.

4. Miter the corners: Fold in from the middle and staple.

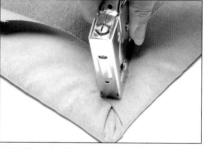
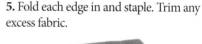

5. Fold each edge in and staple. Trim any excess fabric.

1 HOW TO make a plain loop

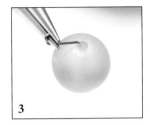

1. If you are making a plain loop above a bead, trim the end of the wire to ⅜ in. (1 cm). Bend it at a right angle against the bead. If you are making a plain loop at the end of a wire, grasp the wire with chainnose pliers ⅜ in. from the end. Make a right-angle bend.

2. Grasp the tip of the wire with your roundnose pliers and feel to be sure that the wire is flush with the edge of the pliers. If you feel a stub of wire, you've grasped too far away from the tip; adjust the pliers.

3. Gently roll the wire until you can't roll comfortably.

4. Reposition the pliers, checking that the fit is snug against the jaw, and continue to roll the loop. The tip of the wire should meet the corner of your initial bend, and you should have a perfect, centered wire circle.

2 HOW TO make a wrapped loop

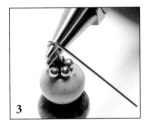

1. To make a wrapped loop above a bead, trim the wire 1¼ in. (3.2 cm) above the bead. Grasp the wire with chainnose pliers above the bead. Fold the wire over the pliers into a right-angle bend. If you're working with just wire (no bead), grasp the wire about 1¼ in. from the end and make a right-angle bend over the pliers.

2. Switch to roundnose pliers. Position the jaws in the bend.

3. Bring the end of the wire up and over the top jaw and as far down as possible.

4. Reposition the pliers so the lower jaw is in the loop. Slide the wire until is it snug on the jaw to be sure that you are working in the same place as in Step 2. Bend the wire down and around the bottom jaw of the pliers until the tail is at a right angle to the neck of the loop. This is called "the first half of a wrapped loop." At this stage, you can connect the loop to another component, such as a chain link or bead dangle.

5. To finish the wrapped loop, switch back to chainnose pliers. Position the pliers' jaw across the loop, as shown.

6. Use a second pair of pliers—roundnose or chainnose—to grasp the wire at the end. Begin to wrap the end around the exposed neck. One wrap will secure the loop, but several wraps look nicer. Be sure to fill in the entire gap between the loop and the bead so the bead is secure. Trim the end and use chainnose pliers to press it close to the wraps.

3 HOW TO open and close a jump ring or plain loop

1

2

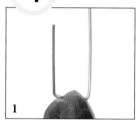

3

1. To open a ring or loop, grasp it with two pairs of pliers held parallel to each other as shown.

2. Bring one pair of pliers toward you and push the other pair away from you.

3. String materials on the open ring or loop as desired. To close, reverse the steps above.

4 HOW TO wrap above a top-drilled bead

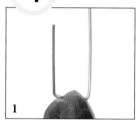

1

2

3

4

1. Cut a 3-in. (7 cm) length of wire, and center a top-drilled bead on the wire. Bend each side upward to form a squared-off U-shape. Leave a tiny bit of room for the bead to move—about 1 mm.

2. Cross the wires into an "X" shape above the bead.

3. Use chainnose pliers to bend one wire straight up and one wire to the side. They'll form a right angle at their intersection.

4. Wrap the horizontal wire around the vertical wire as in a wrapped loop. Make two or three wraps and trim the wire.

5 HOW TO flatten a crimp

1

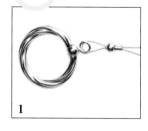

2

1. Hold the crimp tube using the tip of chainnose pliers. Squeeze the pliers firmly to flatten the crimp.

2. Tug the clasp to be sure the crimp has a solid grip.

6 HOW TO attach a fold-over crimp end

1. Glue one end of the cord and place it in a crimp end. Use chainnose pliers to fold one side of the crimp end over the cord.

2. Fold the second side over the first and squeeze gently.

7 HOW TO make a folded crimp

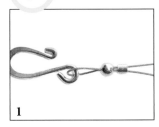

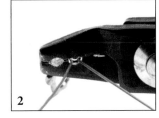

1. On flexible beading wire, string a crimp tube, a spacer, and half the clasp. Bring the wire end back through the beads just strung and pull on the end to tighten the wire.

2. Position the crimp tube in the notch closest to the pliers' handles. Separate the wires, and firmly squeeze the crimp.

3. Place the crimp vertically in the notch at the pliers' tip.

4. Squeeze the crimp, folding it in half at the indentation made in Step 1. Check that the crimp is secure.

8 HOW TO tie an overhand knot

Make a loop and pass the working end through it. Pull the end to tighten the knot.

9 HOW TO tie a surgeon's knot

Cross the right end over the left end and go under and over the cord. Go over and under again. Cross the left end over the right end and go through once. Pull the ends to tighten the knot.

10 HOW TO tie a square knot

Bring the left-hand cord over the right-hand cord and around. Cross right over left, and go through the loop with each end.

Creativity Tips

At this point, I'm hoping that your head is spinning with new ideas. But what happens when you've been beading for a while, and you just can't conjure the muse?

10 tips for getting past a creative dead end

1 Pick a project from this book, or a magazine, or buy a kit, and make the project according to the directions as they are written—no shortcuts. This will force you to think like another designer, and a slightly different approach to a project can teach you a few things.

2 Take a walk, ride your exercise bike, or even do a sink-load of dishes by hand. The repetitive motion of the mindless task will let your mind wander, and you may just stumble onto your path out of your roadblock.

3 Try a small project in a new hobby—if you bead, sew something. If you paint, try polymer clay. Working in a similar, but new-to-you medium may help you look at the same-old-same-old (color blending, for example) in a new way.

4 Make a gift. Choose colors for your friend, not for you. Think of your friend as you work. Consider her colors, her size, her preferences. Your gift will come from the heart, and you may find that thinking away from your own style will reignite your creativity.

5 Accept a commission. Kind of like #4, making something to someone else's specifications will make you consider new materials, new combinations, and new approaches.

6 Look through pictures of your old work (you do take pictures of your masterpieces before you release them, don't you??). When I'm on a jewelry-making roll, something kind of takes over, and I make things I really had no prior plans for. Call it my muse. When I look back at old work, sometimes I think, "Wow. That was really good, and I hardly remember making it."

7 Get thee to a city. For me, it's Milwaukee's Third Ward, or preferably, Chicago. I love my country life, but a few times a year I need to see the crowds, check out what people are really wearing, and see what's in the stores. I'm instantly refreshed and ready to get going again.

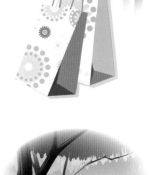

8 If you're a city-dweller, come on out to the country. The rolling landscape, even in winter, can be quite inspiring. Even in the dreary midwinter, I can see more than seven shades of brown outside my window.

9 If you can't get to the city or the country, go ahead and watch some TV. Now, I'm not a big fan of TV, and I went several years without seeing an episode of everyone's favorite Sunday-night drama. However, when I finally turned it on, I smacked my forehead. What a great source for fashion and jewelry inspiration! The same can be said for lots of sitcoms and even the nightly news.

10 Just do it. Jump in, get going, bite off more than you can chew. You'll never get anywhere if you don't get started. Even if you have to undo everything you've done, doing something is much better than doing nothing.

Resources

The first place I shop for materials is at my local bead shop—I'm lucky to have several nearby. Whether you're matching colors or in the early stage of planning a project, there's nothing like seeing the beads in person. Craft and discount stores also are excellent sources for beading materials, especially cords, ribbons, charms, and other findings. Online shopping is an alternative, especially when time is on your side and you're ordering something that you don't need to see up close.

My local bead shops

Eclectica Beads
eclecticabeads.com

Midwest Bead & Supply
midwestbeads.biz

Nottingham Beads
nottinghambeads.com

Craft stores

A.C. Moore
acmoore.com

Jo-Ann Fabric and Crafts
joann.com

Hobby Lobby
hobbylobby.com

Michaels
michaels.com

A few online sources I've had great luck using

Artbeads
artbeads.com

Auntie's Beads
auntiesbeads.com

ebeads.com

Fire Mountain Gems and Beads
firemountaingems.com

Fusion Beads
fusionbeads.com

House of Gems
houseofgems.com

Rings & Things
rings-things.com

Wired Up Beads
wiredupbeads.com

From the Author

When I was young, we would go to my grandmother's beach house for a long vacation every summer. Sunny days were spent collecting rocks, shells, and beach glass. And rainy days? We made jewelry. We saved up our allowance and spent it at a wonderful store with bins of beads. Necessity was the mother of invention; knowing nothing about wrapping loops or folding crimps, we combined simple knots with beads and beach treasures and were very happy with our vacation jewelry.

Fast-forward about 30 years, and I found myself in a new job as an associate editor at a brand-new magazine called *BeadStyle*. I was delighted to blend my love of writing with my love of creating. And I was equally delighted to learn that there was a method to the madness of this wonderful hobby. There were basic techniques to learn! I quickly found out that—as in any hobby—mastering the basics is the most important of all. Once I learned one thing, it seemed I had a million questions about the next thing. All of those questions, and the answers provided by my patient and knowledgeable coworkers, became the foundation of this book. Although I didn't stay at the magazine, I continued to make jewelry for myself and for others. It remains my primary hobby today.

I love to teach, and I especially love helping people who are just discovering this wonderful hobby. Writing books has helped me reach a greater audience. *Mostly Metals: A Beginner's Guide to Designing Jewelry* and *Altered You! Alter Your Style, Your Stuff, Your Space* were published in 2008. My blog (www.artfulcrafts.blogspot.com) lets me explore and share projects in a more immediate way.

Acknowledgments

My family remains the center of my universe. My thanks go to Meredith and Haley, for understanding and putting up with the chaos that comes from writing a book in my "free" time, and to Steve, for his unconditional love and support, no matter what zigzagging path I choose to follow. Thanks to my publisher for the opportunity to participate in this exciting series, the oh-so-fabulous art and photography team, and to my editor, Mary Wohlgemuth, whose masterful stewardship brought this project from loose pages and stray jewelry into the book you hold today.